CONTENTS

Published by Coordination Group Publications Ltd.

Contributors:
Charley Darbishire, Simon Little, Iain Nash,
Andy Park, Glenn Rogers, Claire Thompson

Consultant:
Maf Gibbons

ISBN: 978 1 84146 459 6
Groovy website: www.cgpbooks.co.uk

Printed by Elanders Hindson Ltd, Newcastle upon Tyne.
Clipart sources: CorelDRAW® and VECTOR.
With thanks to Microsoft, Logotron and Expressive Software Projects for permission to use screenshots from MS Word and Outlook Express, Junior ViewPoint and Compose World Junior respectively.

The Basics of Windows

Here's a bit of easy stuff to start you off.

Title Bar

The title bar tells you the name of the program and the file. You can move the window around by dragging the title bar.

Window Buttons

This button shrinks the window and puts it at the bottom.

This one closes the window.

This one makes it fill the screen. (Click again to get the window back to the size it was before.)

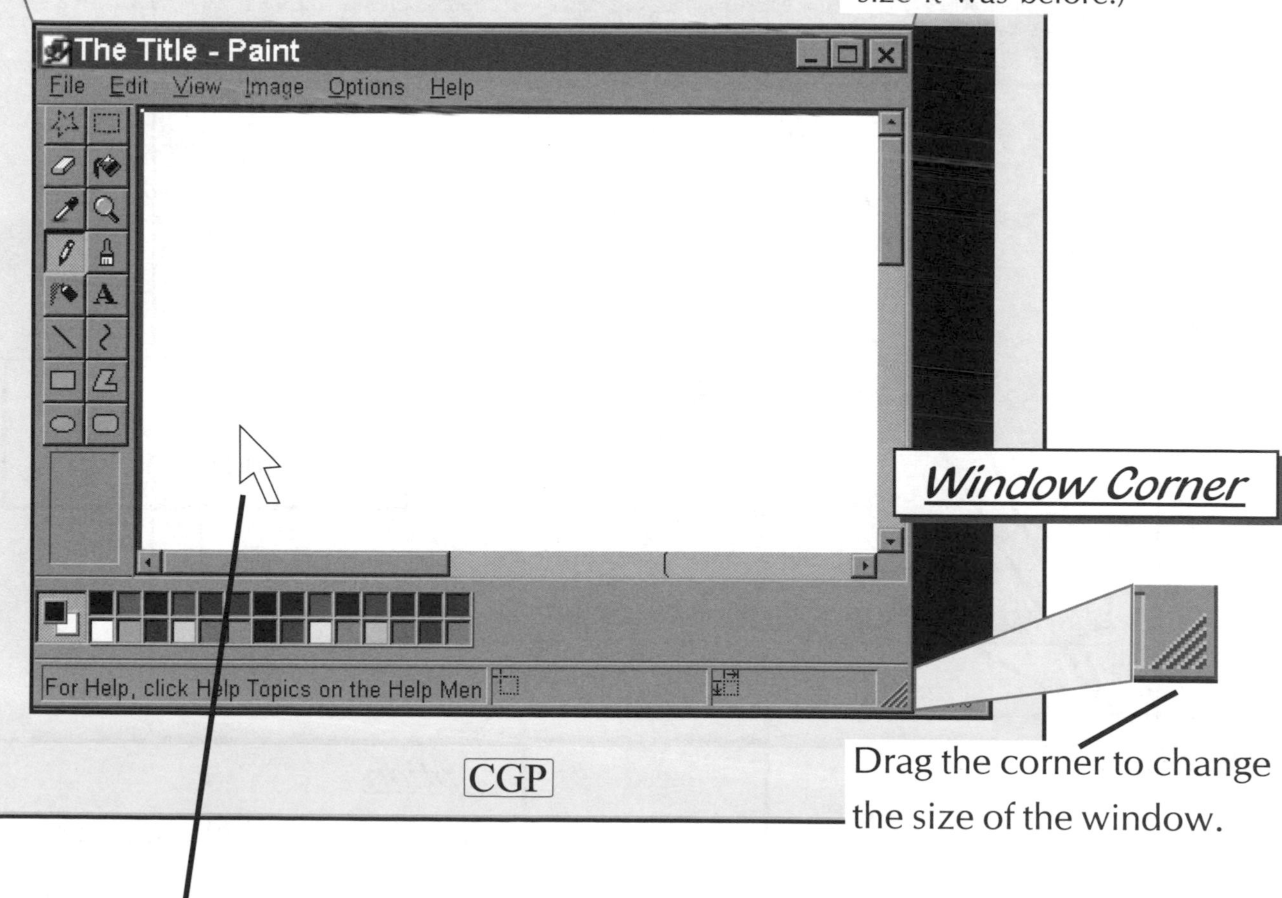

Window Corner

Drag the corner to change the size of the window.

Pointer

The pointer is the thing you move with your mouse.
(In word-processing programs it's called a cursor and looks like this: I)

Word Processed Pages

When you type something on a computer, you make a document.
Here are some things you need to know about documents.

You need to know about all the bits on the page

This is a short poem done in Microsoft Word.
I've pointed out all the bits you need to know about.

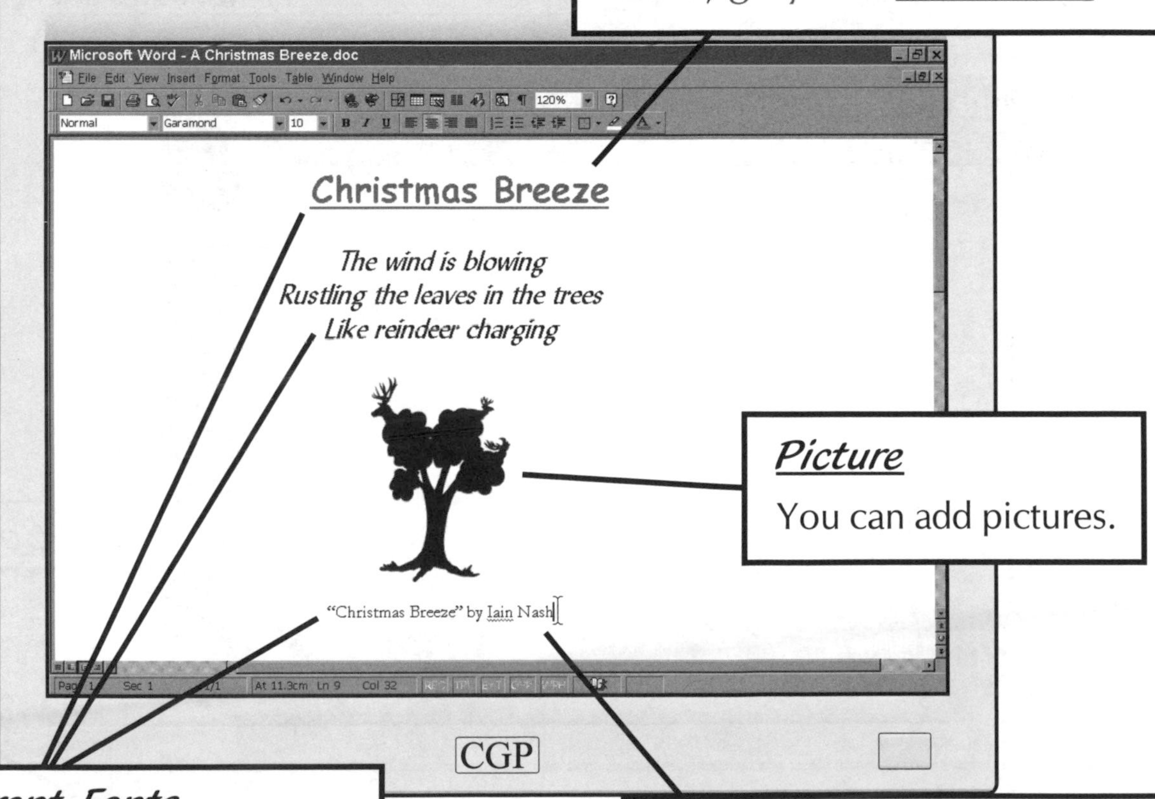

Title

The title is at the top.
It needs to stand out — here, it's **bold**, grey and underlined.

Picture

You can add pictures.

Different Fonts

The font is the shape of the letters. You can use different fonts for different bits.

Caption

A caption is a label under a picture.
It tells you what the picture is about.

There's loads of funky stuff you can do to text. It's great. ☺

Word Processed Pages

① Where should a title go?

....

② Name three ways you can make a title stand out.

1. ....

2. ....

3. ....

③ Here is a birthday card. Which bits are which?

Fill in the labels using these words:

MESSAGE TITLE POEM CAPTION

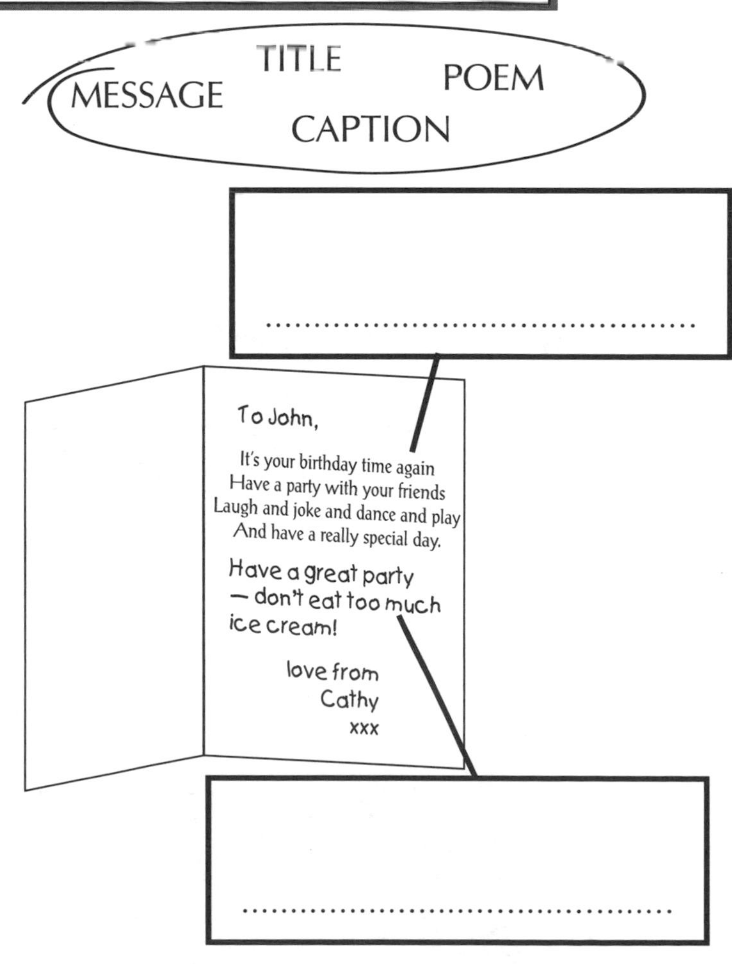

Highlighting Text

On a computer, you need to highlight things before you can change them.

Here are three ways to HIGHLIGHT words

A Windy Conversation

"The wind is blowing," said Helga.
"Yes, it's rustling the leaves in the trees," said Elma.
"It sounds like reindeer charging," commented Helga.

CLICK AND DRAG

Hold the left mouse button down and drag the cursor to 'highlight' something.

DOUBLE CLICK

'Double-click' to highlight a whole word.

A Windy Conversation

"The wind is blowing," said Helga.
"Yes, it's rustling the leaves in the trees," said Elma.
"It sounds like reindeer charging," commented Helga.

SELECT ALL

'Select all' highlights everything on the page.
It's in the **Edit menu** at the top of the screen.

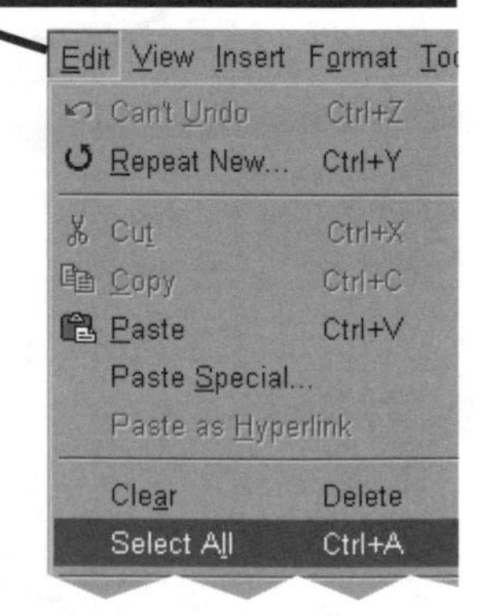

A Windy Conversation

"The wind is blowing," said Helga.
"Yes, it's rustling the leaves in the trees," said Elma.
"It sounds like reindeer charging," commented Helga.

Hey smartypants...

A triple-click will select the whole paragraph.

Highlighting Text

① What do you need to do before you can change text?

....

② Join these up to what they do.

SELECT ALL

DOUBLE CLICK

CLICK AND DRAG

Highlights where the cursor goes.

Highlights everything on the page.

Selects a whole word.

③ How do I change the title of this story?

I want to change the title to "An Amazing Rocket Trip".
Which of these should I do?

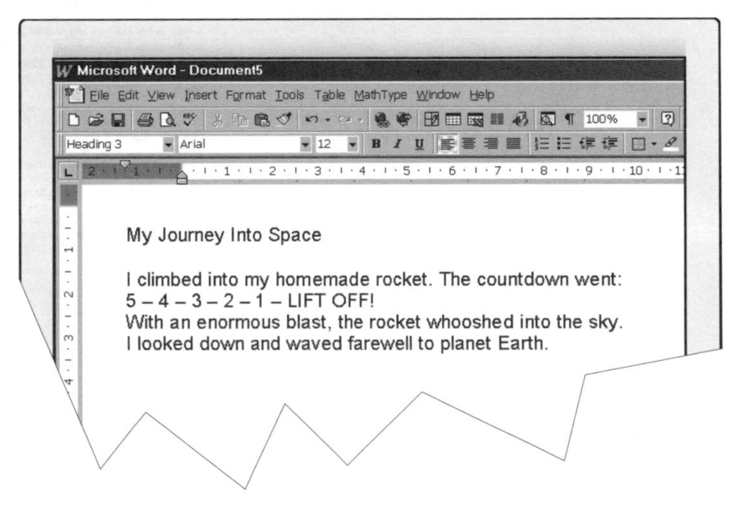

A **Double-click** on "Journey", then type the new title.

B Go to the Edit menu and choose **select all**, then type the new title.

C **Click and Drag** the cursor across the title, then type the new title.

The answer is ☐.

Copying and Pasting Text

HIGHLIGHTING text allows you to COPY it

There's an easy way to repeat something you've typed.

Copy picks up a **copy** of the text

1. Highlight the words you want to repeat.
2. Click on Edit.
3. Click on Copy.

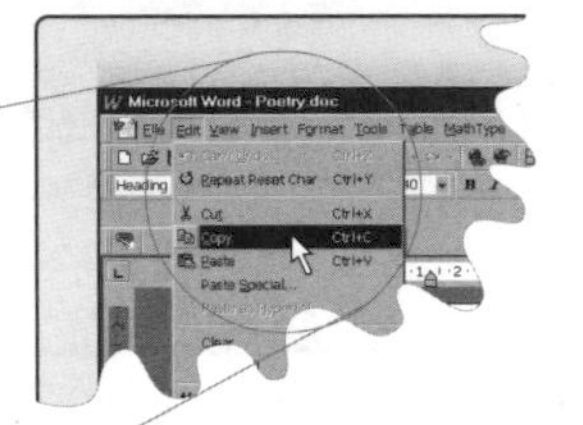

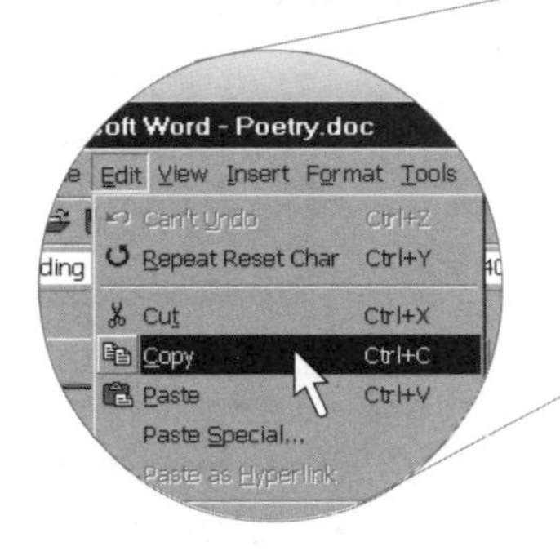

Copy stores the words ready to put them down again.

Paste puts it down wherever you want it

Click where you want the copied text to go then click 'Paste' to place the copy.

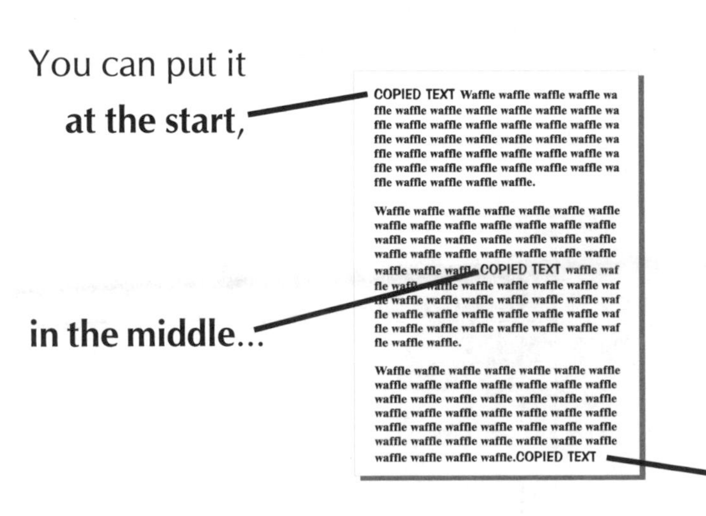

...or **at the end**.

You can copy and paste text

— in the same file,
— from one file to another,
— from one program to another.

Copying and Pasting Text

① Fill in the blanks using these words:

Paste
cursor
copy

Clicking on "Edit" then "Copy" picks up a .... of the highlighted text.

Clicking on "........................" places the text you copied.

The text is repeated wherever the .... is.

② Tick the right box to say if these are true or false.

	True	False
You can copy and paste text inside the same file.	☐	☐
You can copy and paste text from file to file.	☐	☐
You can copy and paste text from your computer to your text book.	☐	☐
You can copy and paste text from program to program.	☐	☐
You can paste the text onto your grandma's cat.	☐	☐

Changing dull words

You'll need a word-processing program for this bit.
(If you're lucky, someone might do the typing for you.)

In this Project You Will:

Here is some writing about snails:

Copy it out

1) Open your writing program.
2) Copy this out into a blank file.

Press enter twice after the title to make this space.

Collecting Snails

I have a nice hobby. I collect snails.
Stacy is my favourite snail.
She is a nice brown colour.
I wish I were a snail.
It would be a nice life.
But one day, a nice bird would eat me.

CGP

Choose different words instead of "nice"

The passage uses the word **"nice"** too many times. This makes it boring.

Think of better words to replace each "nice".
Write them in the boxes.

Some words that you could use:
strange *big* *pale*
lazy *hungry*

I have a nice hobby. I collect nice snails.
Stacy is my favourite snail.
She is a nice brown colour.
I wish I were a snail.
It would be a nice life.
But one day, a nice bird would eat me.

Changing dull words

Now you can put the new words in

1) **Double-click** on the first "nice" to highlight it. Like this: nice
2) **Type** in the new word. It will replace the old word.
3) Do the same for the other words.

Extra Bits for you to Try:

Change the title

1) Can you think of a **better title** than "Collecting Snails"? Write it here:

....

2) Now **highlight** the title.

Collecting Snails

Hold down the left mouse button and **drag** the cursor across the title.

3) **Type in** your new title.

Save your work

1) Go to the File menu and choose Save.
2) You will need to choose a filename.

Write the name of the file here:

What is the Font?

You can easily make text look different by using different fonts.

'Font' Describes How the Letters Look

Here is a poem title in different fonts: These are the font names:

A Christmas Breeze — Seagull Hv BT

A Christmas Breeze — Harrington

A Christmas Breeze — Bradley Hand ITC

A Christmas Breeze — AdLib BT

The font is in a menu at the top of the screen

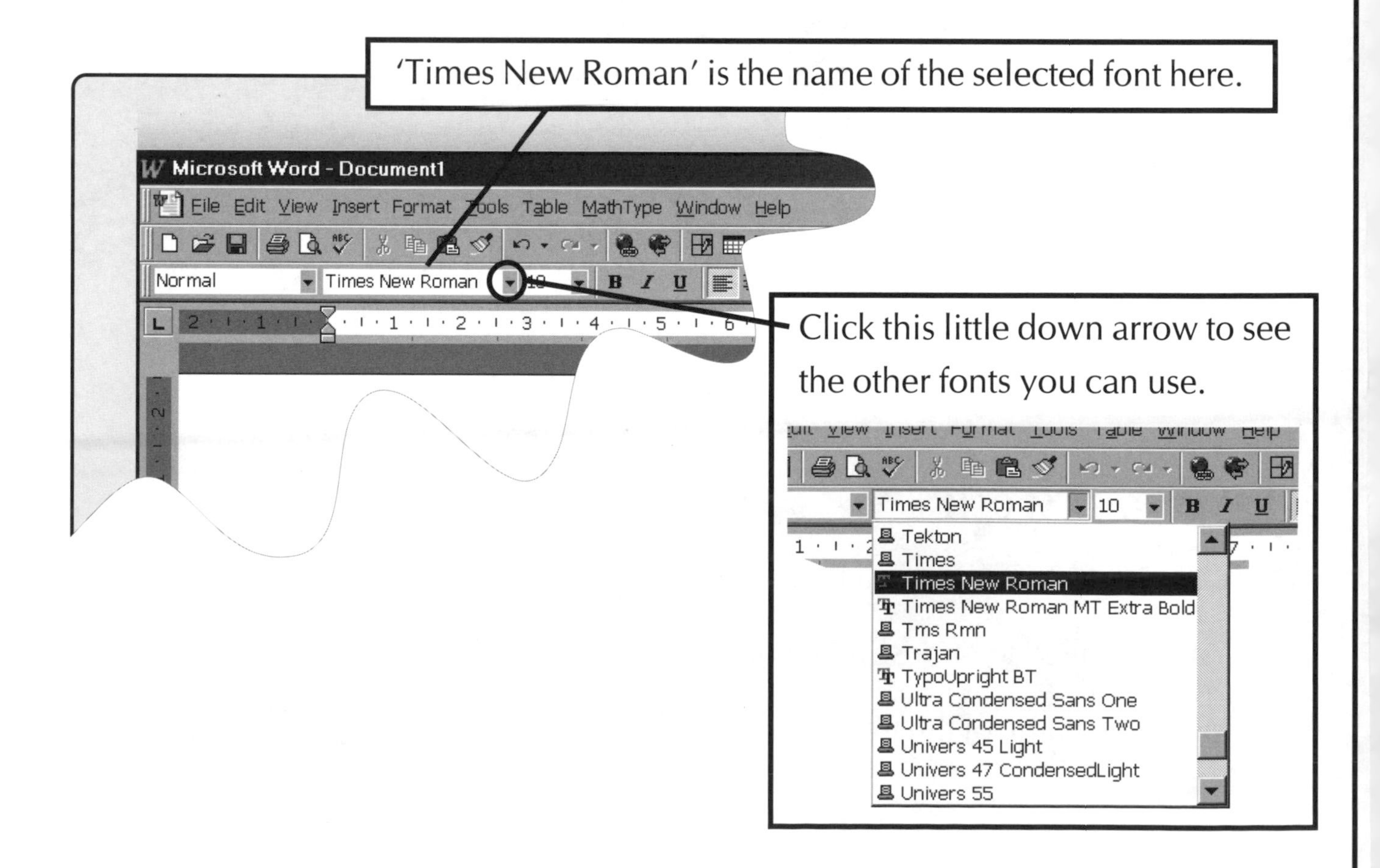

What is the Font?

① What is an easy way to make text look different?

....

② What name is given to how the letters look?

☐ Font ☐ Fanta

☐ Felt ☐ Fred

③ What do you do if you want to see the list of fonts?

....

④ Find a way through the maze, then finish off the sentence below.

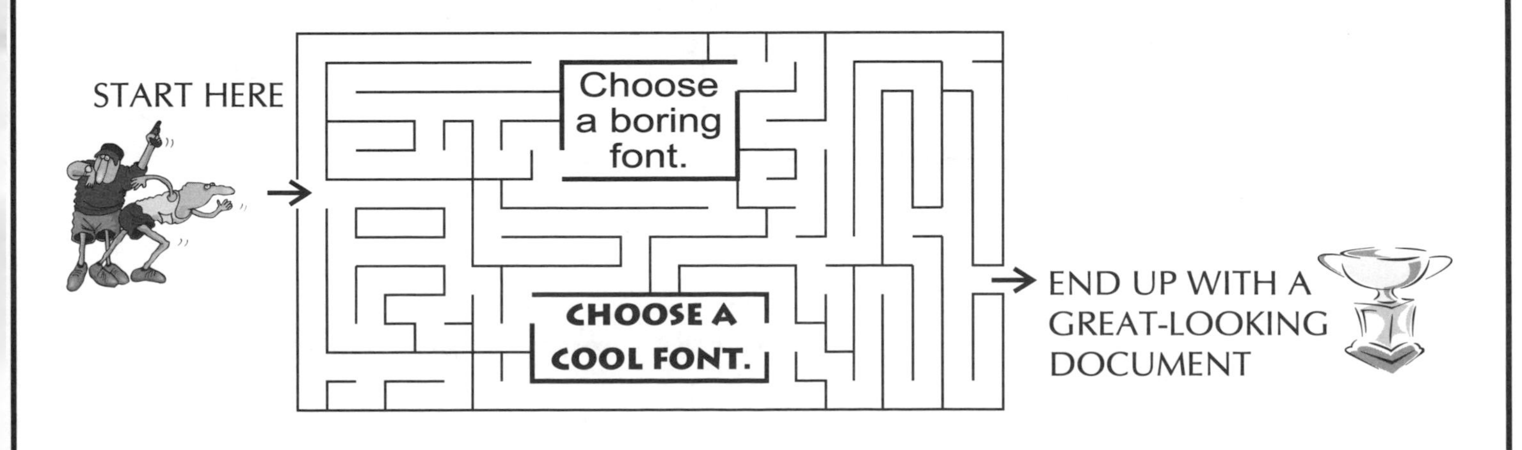

To get a great-looking document you have to choose a .... font.

Changing How the Words Look

The toolbar at the top of the screen lets you change the way the words look.

The Text Toolbar looks like this...

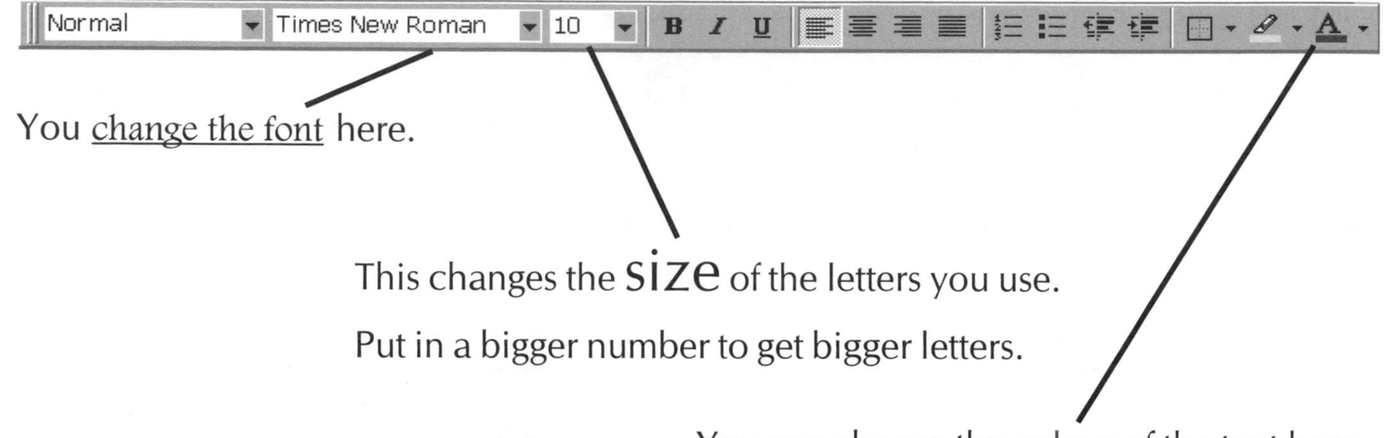

You change the font here.

This changes the size of the letters you use.

Put in a bigger number to get bigger letters.

You can choose the colour of the text here.

Highlight words before you change them

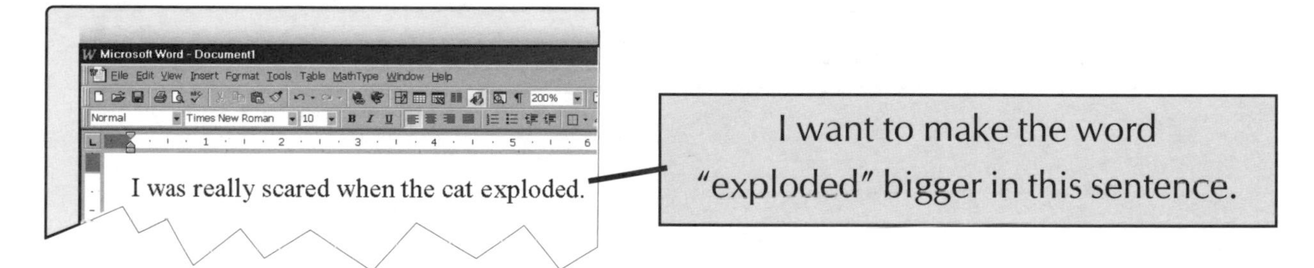

I want to make the word "exploded" bigger in this sentence.

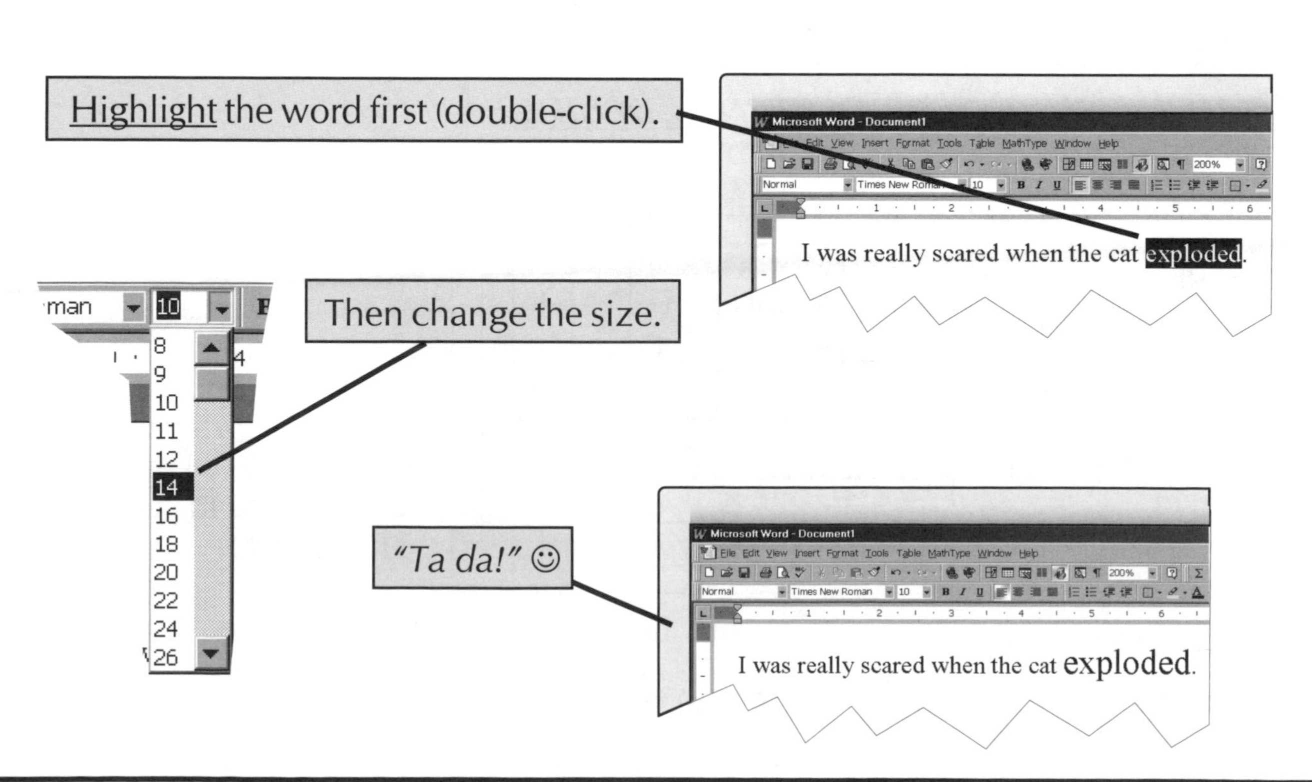

Highlight the word first (double-click).

Then change the size.

"Ta da!" ☺

Changing How the Words Look

① How do you change the font?

Tick ✔ the one correct answer.

- Click on this and choose a new font from the menu. ☐
  Normal
- Click on this and choose a new font from the menu. ☐
  Times New Roman
- Click on this and choose a new font from the menu. ☐
  A
- Ask Freda the cow to do it. ☐

② Choose the right word to complete these sentences.

colour **moo** **bigger** **smaller**

To make the text bigger, click on this and choose a .... number.

10

To change the ...., click on this and choose a different one.

A

To win the lottery, click on Freda the cow and say ".............................."

③ Before you change a word, you must...

☐ copy it ☐ highlight it ☐ ask Freda

Tick ✔ the correct answer.

Decorating the Words

Here are some more ways to change how your words look.

*You make words **stand out**, using the B, I, and U buttons*

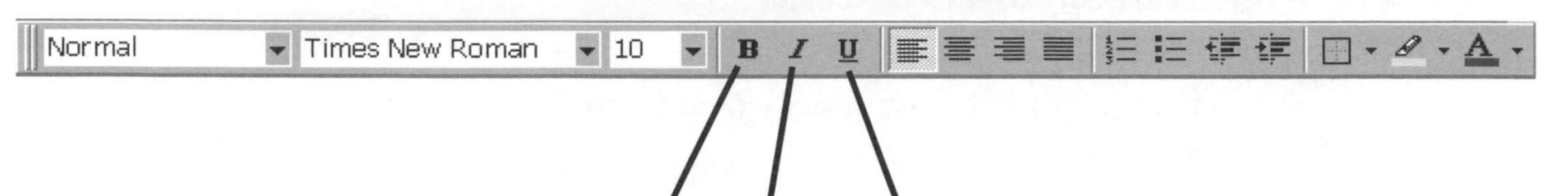

These three buttons make your text **bold**, *italic*, or underlined. ***Or all three!***

This text is bold. *This text is italic.* This text is underlined.

This text is all three.

WordArt lets you do some great effects

Most word processor programs let you do stuff like this:

In Microsoft Word, it's called WordArt.

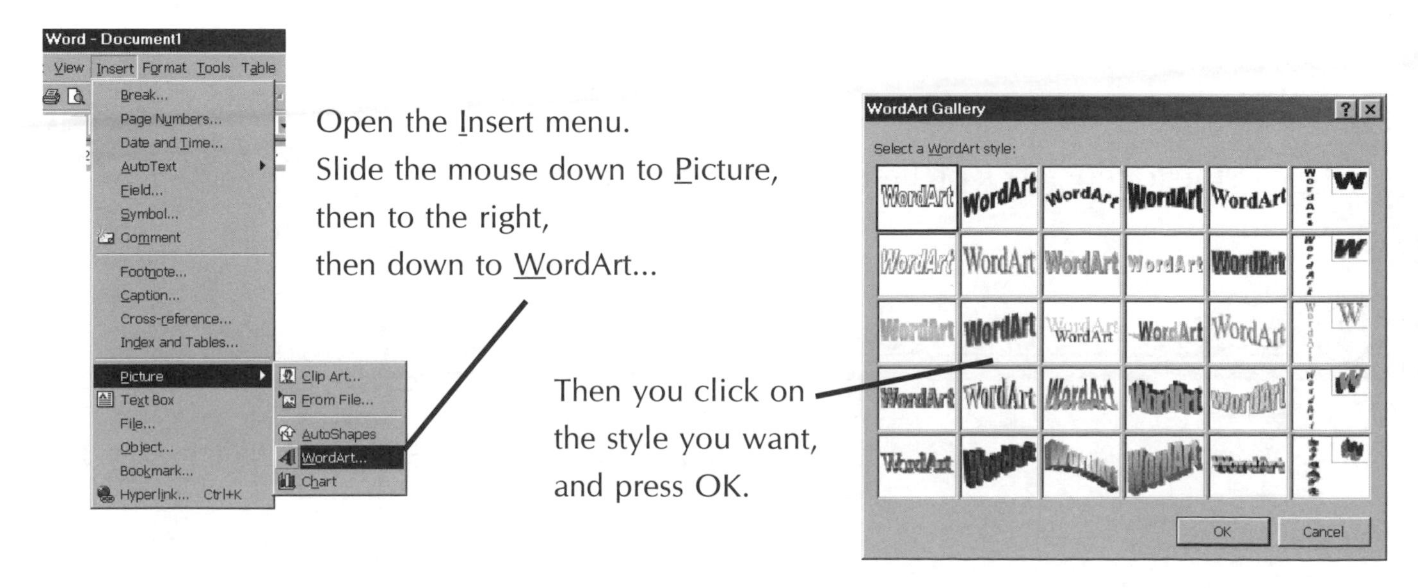

Open the Insert menu.
Slide the mouse down to Picture,
then to the right,
then down to WordArt...

Then you click on the style you want, and press OK.

Decorating the Words

① Fill in these sentences.

a) Clicking **B** will make the text bold.

b) Clicking *I* will make the text ....

c) Clicking U will make the text ....

② Pick out the bold and italic words.

"I have *never* seen such a scary octopus," said Fred the Pilchard. "This looks like a job for **Supercod**."

The bold word is ....

The italic word is ....

③ Can you match the WordArt styles together?

Draw a line from the words on the left to the correct box.

I love knitting

Hedgehog

Squishy tomatoes

Playing with the layout

Alignment is where the words line up on the page.

You can change the ALIGNMENT of the text

There might be buttons to do this on the toolbar.

They usually look a bit like this

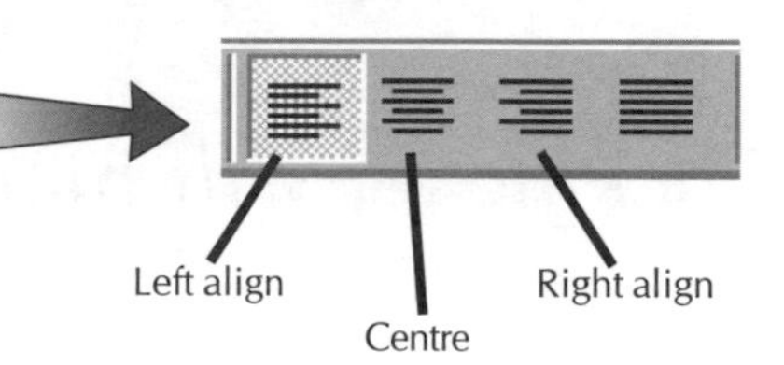

This text is on the left

This text is **left align**ed. This text is **left align**ed.
This text is **left align**ed. This text is
left aligned.
This text is **left align**ed.

This text is on the right

This text is **right align**ed. This text is **right align**ed.
This text is **right align**ed. This text is
right aligned.
This text is **right align**ed.

This text is in the middle

This text is **centre align**ed. This text is **centre align**ed.
This text is **centre align**ed. This text is
centre aligned.
This text is **centre align**ed.

Hey cleverclogs...

The fourth button is "justify".

It makes the text fit neatly to either side of the page.

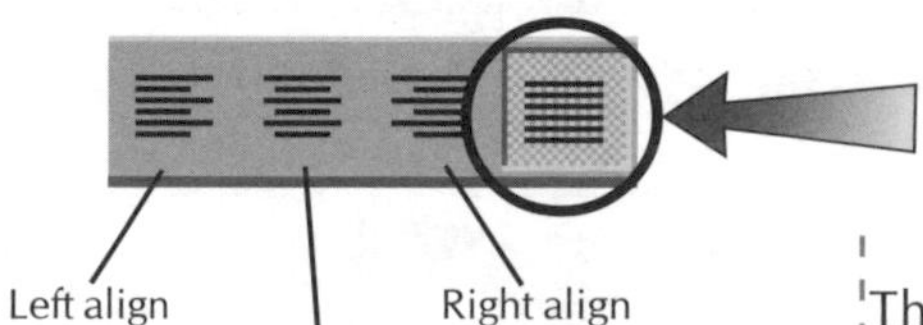

This text is **justified**. This text is **justified**. This text is **justified**. This text is **justified**. This text is **justified**. This text is **justified**. This text is **justified**. This text is **justified**. This text is **justified**. This text is **justified**. This text is **justified**.

Playing with the layout

① What does alignment mean?

Alignment is what you do when you...

- ☐ change where the text lines up on the page.
- ☐ queue at McDonald's.
- ☐ change the font.
- ☐ underline something.

② Draw a line from each button to what it does to text.

Centre button icon		Right align
Justify button icon (I've done this one for you. →)	— line drawn to Justify —	Left align
Left align button icon		Justify
Right align button icon		Centre

③ Is this text justified?

One of these passages is justified. (The other one is right-aligned.)

Write a "J" in the box next to the text that's **justified**.

☐ The frog leapt onto Gemma's head. Then it leapt onto Andy's head. Then onto Claire's head, then Iain's head, then Simon's head. Finally, it leapt into the pond.

Gemma jumped into the pond. Then Andy jumped into pond. Claire and Iain jumped into the pond. Simon fell into the pond. ☐

For this activity, you need a wordprocessor with simple text editing features.

In this activity you will:

Change the size

1. Open a blank file in your writing program.
2. Type in the word "grow".
3. Change the size of each letter so the word gets bigger.

   g r o W

4. Now type the word "shrink" and make it get smaller.

   S h r i n k

Change colours

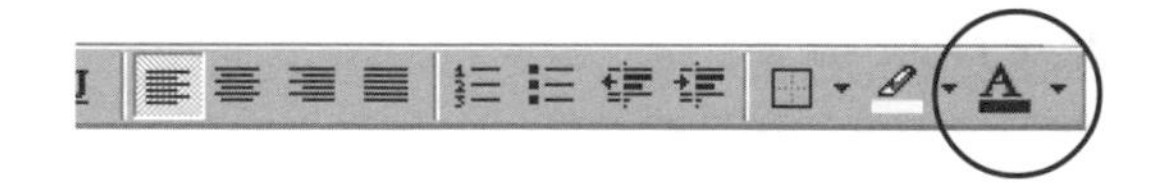

1. Think of something red. (I thought of blood!)
2. Type it in and then **change the colour** to match it.

   blood

3. Type the word "rainbow".
4. Change the colours of the letters to make it look like a rainbow.

   rainbow

Making the text look cool

Computer Activity

Here is a piece of writing about watering things.

Watering things

People water plants to make them grow.

Some people water evil witches to make them shrivel up.

Clouds water sunshine to make rainbows.

I've changed the size of letters.

I've changed colours.

I've changed the font of words.

Now...

Either do this:

1. Write a short story of your own.
2. Change the size,
   colour,
   and font of different words.

Try to make the words like their meaning.

or do this:

1. Type out the passage above.
2. Try to change the words just like I have.

Don't forget to Save your work

Write the name of the file here:

Inserting Pictures

Pictures make your document look cool.

Pictures can be photos, artwork or cartoons

A photograph

A drawing

A cartoon from Clipart

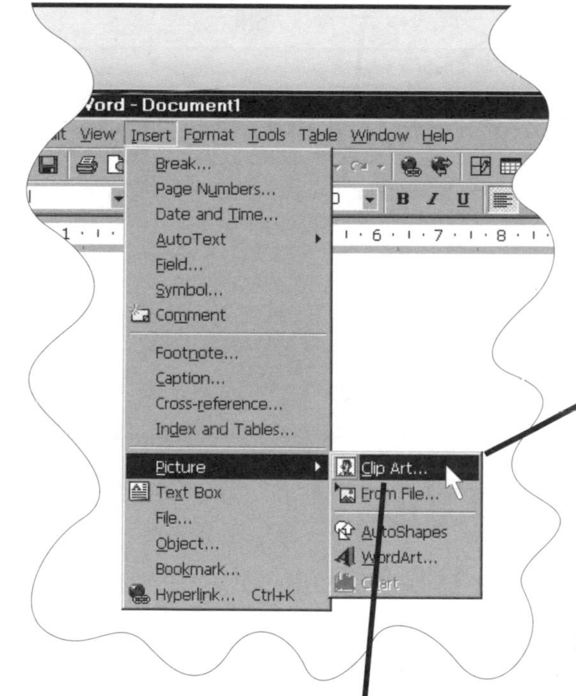

Putting in a Clipart picture

To put in a clipart picture:

Open the 'Insert' menu.
Go to Picture, then to 'Clipart'.

You'll get a menu with loads of pictures to choose from.

Click on the picture you want and press the open or insert button.

Brittany_Spears.jpg

Open

To put in your own picture or photo, choose 'From File...' instead of 'Clip Art'.

You need to know the **filename** of your picture.

Inserting Pictures

① Fill in the blanks.

People put .... in their work because they look ....

② What **three** types of picture are there?

1. ....

2. ....

3. ....

② Cartoon or Photo?

Write 'photo' or 'cartoon' under each of these pictures.

....

③ Which menu do you use to get pictures?

....

④ Choose the right word from the list to fill in the blank.

parents lightswitch habits filename

If you're using a picture 'From File', you need to know the .... of the picture.

Changing the Size of Things

Once the picture's there, it needs to look right.
It needs to be the **right size**.

Click on the picture to make the little squares appear

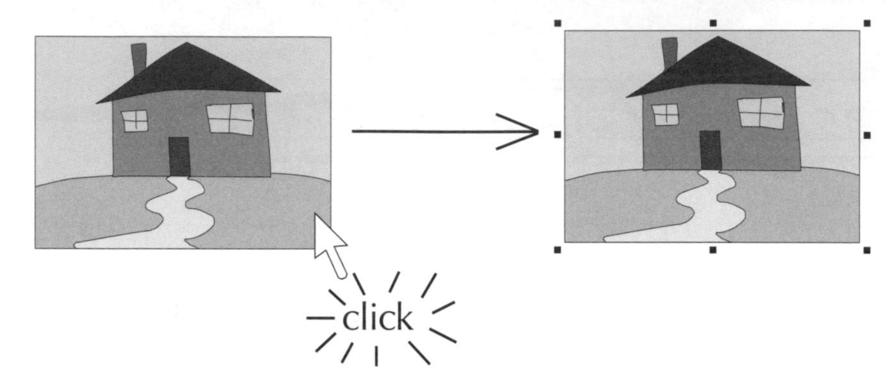

The little squares show you've **selected** the picture. It's just like highlighting text.
The little squares are called <u>handles</u>. They're normally white or black.

The little squares let you ***change the size*** *of the picture*

1. Click on the side ones and drag sideways to **stretch or squash** the picture **sideways**.

2.

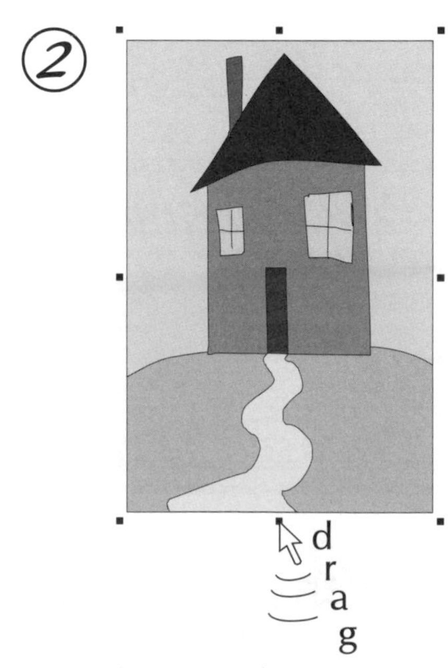

Drag the top or bottom ones up or down to **stretch or squash** the picture **upwards or downwards.**

3.

Drag the corner ones out or in to make the picture **bigger or smaller**.

Changing the Size of Things

① *When you click on a picture...*

☐ it changes the picture into another one.

☐ it gets smaller.

☐ it selects (highlights) the picture so that you can edit it.

☐ the mouse blows up.

Tick ✔ the correct answer.

② *What are the tiny squares round a picture used for?*

Tick ✔ the correct answer.

☐ Changing the size of the picture.

☐ Changing the picture.

☐ Changing the colours in picture.

☐ Opening doors.

③ *Fill in the blanks*

tall, wide, drag, bigger, change

You .... one of the little boxes to .... the size of a picture.

Moving one of the corner boxes makes the picture .... or smaller.

The boxes at the sides change how .... the picture is.

The boxes at the top and bottom change how .... the picture is.

Computer Activity

Using Pictures

You can use one of your own documents for this activity.

In this project you will:

Start with some sentences that need a picture

Write some sentences that you can put a picture to.

Need ideas?

Write about your favourite animal,
or about your favourite sport,
or about something scary.

Or you could **Open** a document you have done before.
Ask someone if you need help with this.

The Eiffel Tower

The Eiffel tower stands
Tall as an Alpine mountain.
But mountains don't rust.

Have a look through Clipart

1. Click the cursor where you want the picture to be.
2. Go to **Clipart** and look through the pictures.

   Use the menus at the top of the page:
   Insert → Picture → Clipart

3. Find a picture that will go well with your document.

This one looks just right!

Using Pictures

Computer Activity 

Insert the picture

1. Write the name of the picture here:

2. Click on the picture and press **insert** or **open** to put it in your document.

This picture looks silly because it's too big.

The Eiffel Tower

The Eiffel tower stands
Tall as an Alpine mountain.
But mountains don't rust.

Change the size of the picture

1. Click on one of the corner squares **of your picture**.
2. Drag the mouse to change the size of the picture. Make the picture the right size for your page.

You can <u>move</u> the picture too — <u>click</u> on it and <u>drag it</u> with the mouse.

The Eiffel Tower

The Eiffel tower stands
Tall as an Alpine mountain.
But mountains don't rust.

Try this

1. Click on and drag one of the **side** squares.
2. Change it back by clicking **Edit** then **Undo**.
3. **Circle** the right word to complete this sentence:

When you drag one of the **side** squares, the picture **stretches** / **explodes**.

Save your work

Write the filename here:

Using Music Software

You can write songs with musical pictures

Music software can make it really easy to compose tunes.
This one's called Compose World Junior.

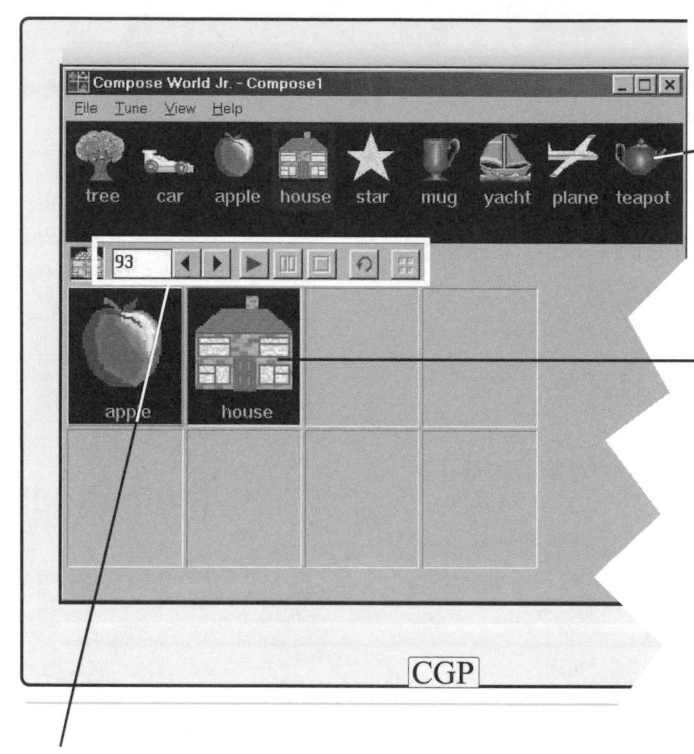

Each picture has a melody to go with it.

You drag the pictures down to make a musical sequence.

Then you just press PLAY to listen to your sequence.

These are the **buttons** you need to play your sequence.

Three great things about programs like this...

Pictures are easy to remember
– it's easy to remember a **tune** when it has a picture.

You can **build** a song in chunks.
It's like using musical building blocks.

You don't have to play the tune yourself.
You just press the **play** button.

Using Music Software

① What do the pictures do?

They make the screen look pretty.

They play different tunes.

They read your thoughts.

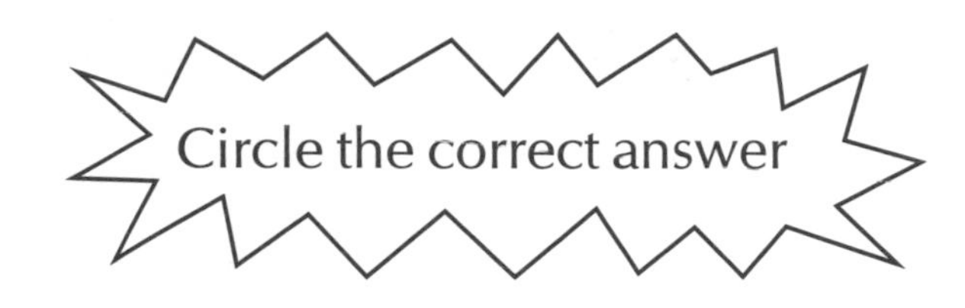

② Can you guess what these buttons do?

Draw tails from the animals to the right buttons.

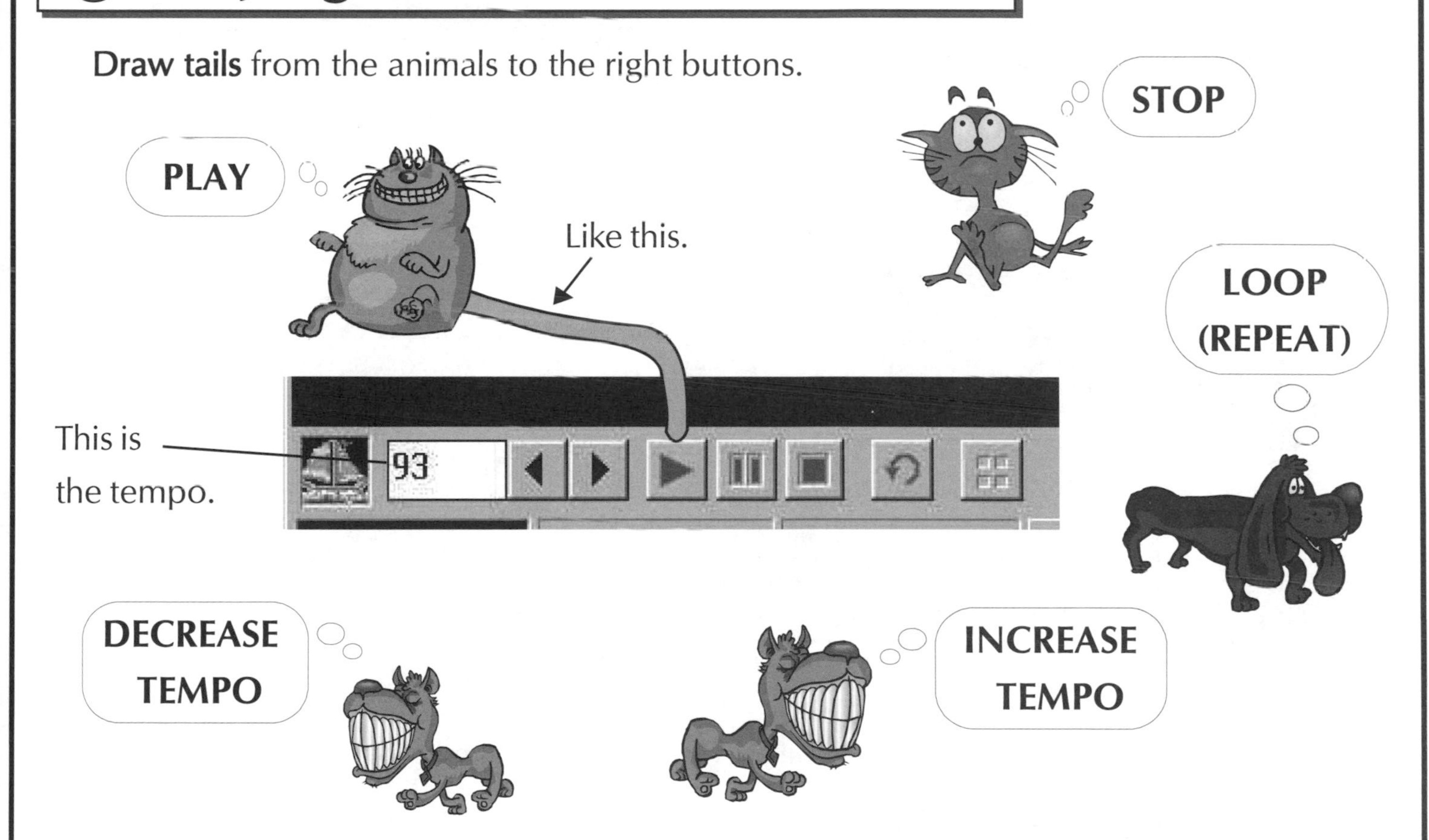

③ Why are music programs that use pictures great?

1. ....

2. ....

3. ....

Changing Your Tune

Here are some ways you can change your tune.

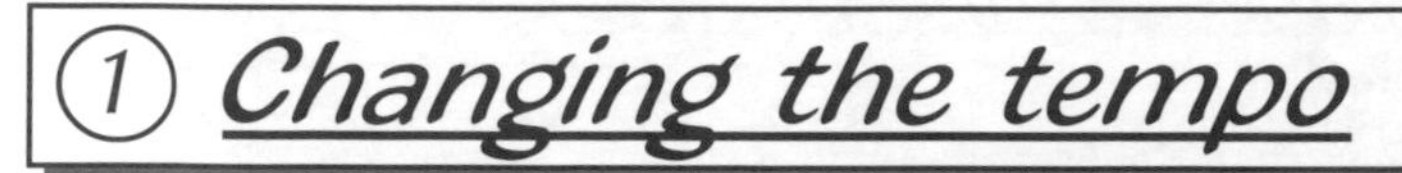

① *Changing the tempo*

Tempo is how fast the music is played.

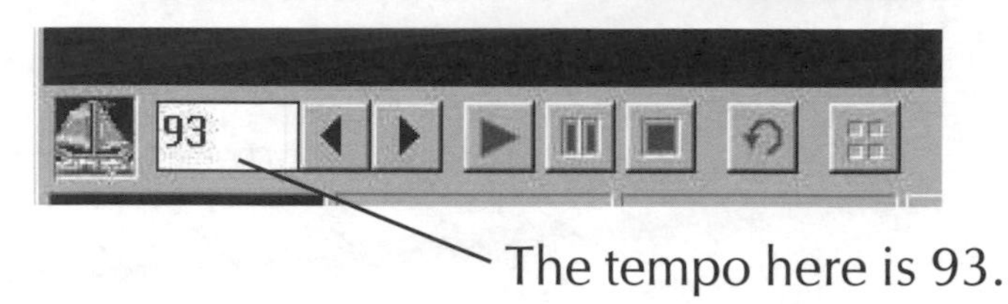

The tempo here is 93.

② *Opening new pictures and music*

On Compose World Junior, go to the <u>File Menu</u> and choose <u>open</u>.

These are all different <u>picture sets</u>.
Each picture set has different music.

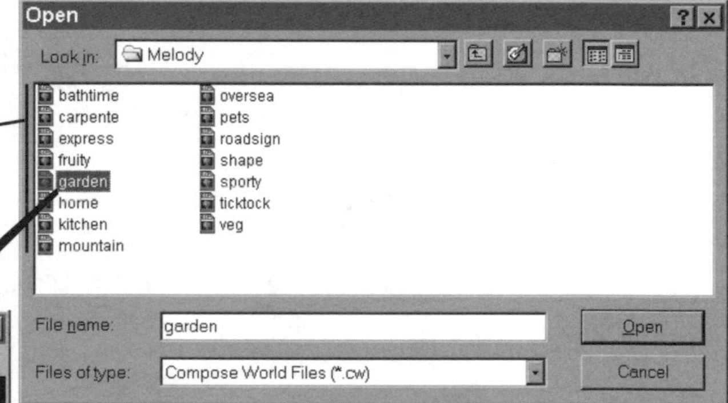

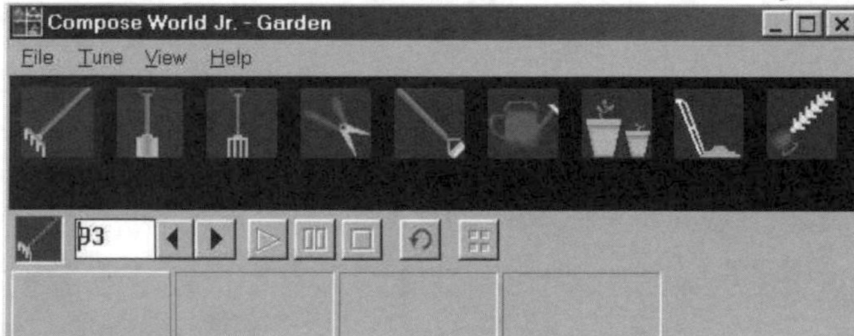

③ *Choosing different instruments*

You can change the instruments used in any sequence.
This means you make your tune sound more how <u>you want it</u> to.

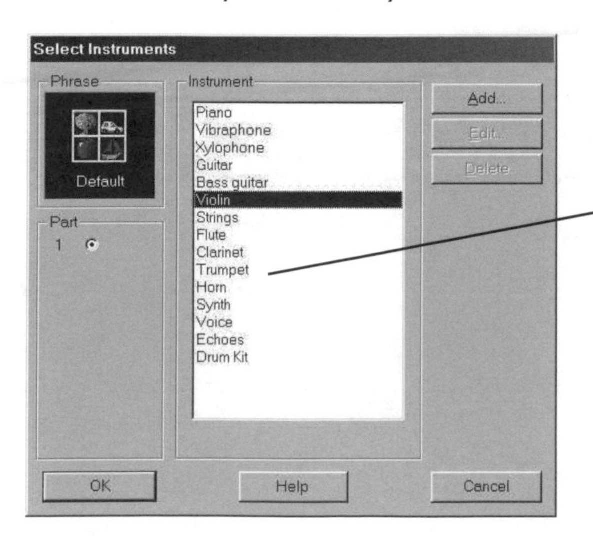

On Compose World Junior, go to the <u>Tunes Menu</u> and select <u>default instruments</u>.

There should be quite a wide range of instruments to choose from like this.

You can make the same tune <u>very different</u> just by changing the instruments.

Changing Your Tune

① What happens when I change the tempo from 80 to 100?

Draw a smelly sock
around the correct answer.

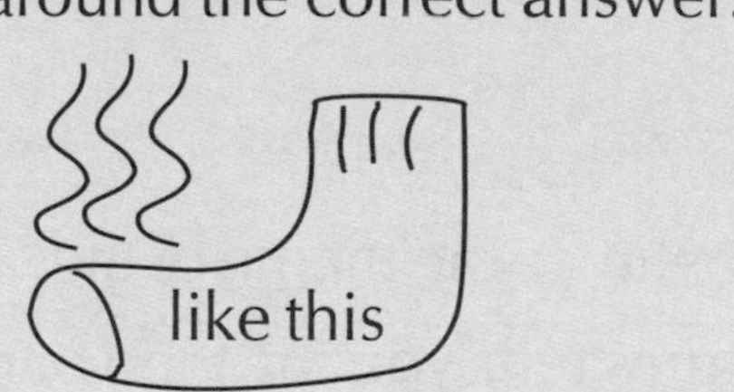

It gets faster.

It gets louder.

Its gets slower.

It gets smellier.

② How do I open the set of pictures called "dreams"?

I've opened this menu. I want the picture set called "dreams".
What should I do now?

A. Click on "dreams", then click **open**.

B. Click on "dreams", then click **cancel**.

C. Type "dreams" here then click **open**.

D. Type "milkshake" and press **yes please**.

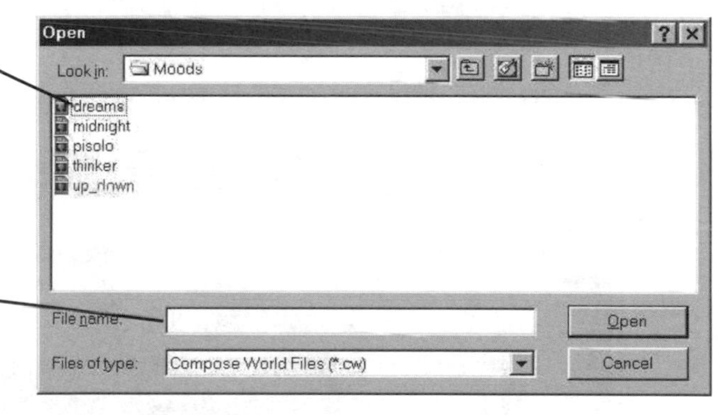

The correct answers are ☐ and ☐ — they both work!

③ Find these six instruments in the word grid

T	H	G	U	I	T	A	R	H	S
P	R	N	T	R	U	M	D	L	P
G	F	J	S	T	K	R	S	Y	I
U	C	L	A	R	I	N	E	T	A
I	H	P	U	U	G	J	L	V	N
T	O	B	J	M	Y	K	E	I	I
A	R	D	O	P	I	A	N	O	V
P	N	A	K	E	S	T	A	L	D
N	F	L	U	T	E	K	N	I	K
V	I	O	S	Y	T	D	O	N	E

Flute

Guitar

Piano

Violin

Clarinet

Trumpet

Using Different Picture Sets

Using the same pictures all the time can get boring.
Here are some different pictures:

① Pictures and Music with the same theme

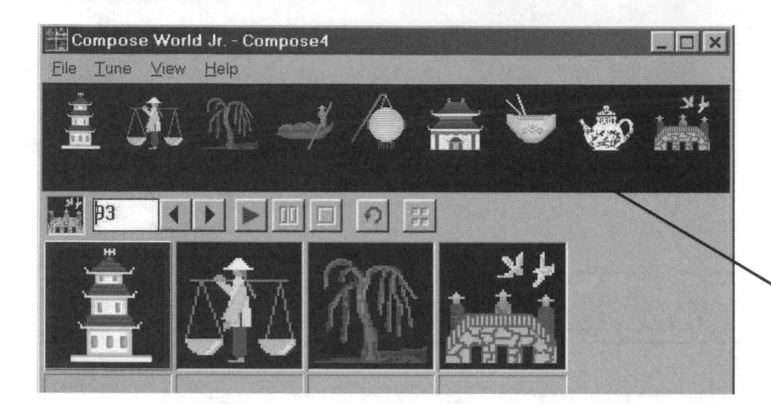

Sometimes the theme of the pictures tells you the kind of music.

The tunes that go with these pictures all sound oriental.

② Pictures that represent different moods

The music for each of these weather pictures matches the mood of the picture.

The music for storm is loud and menacing.

But the music for sunset is quiet and relaxing.

③ Proper Musical Notation

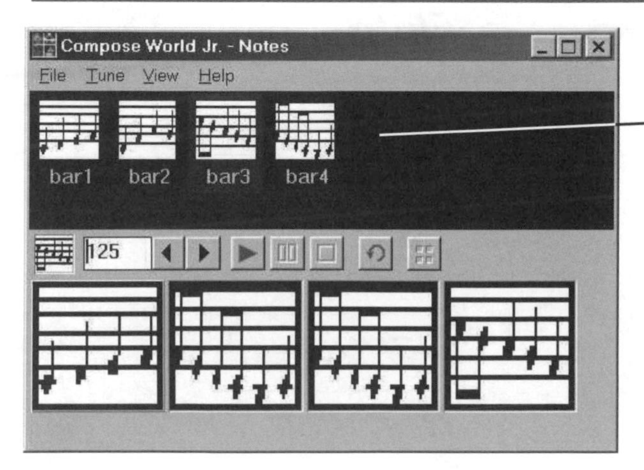

These pictures use proper music notation. They show the actual notes being played.

This is how music is written for most musical instruments.

Using Different Picture Sets

① Choose the best picture set.

Here are three picture sets:

B

C

Choose which you think would be best for:

A spooky haunted house story. 

A story with lots of mood changes. 

Learning what musical chords sound like. 

② Music to fit the mood of the picture.

Below are some more weather pictures.
Describe the kind of sounds that would go with each picture.

Here are some words you could use:

relaxing soft loud whirling
fuzzy crashing booming gentle
whistling tapping slow piercing

Sunny ....

Windy ....

Rainy ....

Lightning ....

Write Your Own Song

In this activity you will:

Making the tune

1. Load up your music program.

2. Now **open a set of pictures** to use.

   You'll probably have to go to the **File** menu at the top of screen and select **Open**.

3. You're going to **create a musical sequence** using four pictures.
   So **drag** four pictures from the top to make a sequence.
   Play about with it until you've got something that sounds ace.

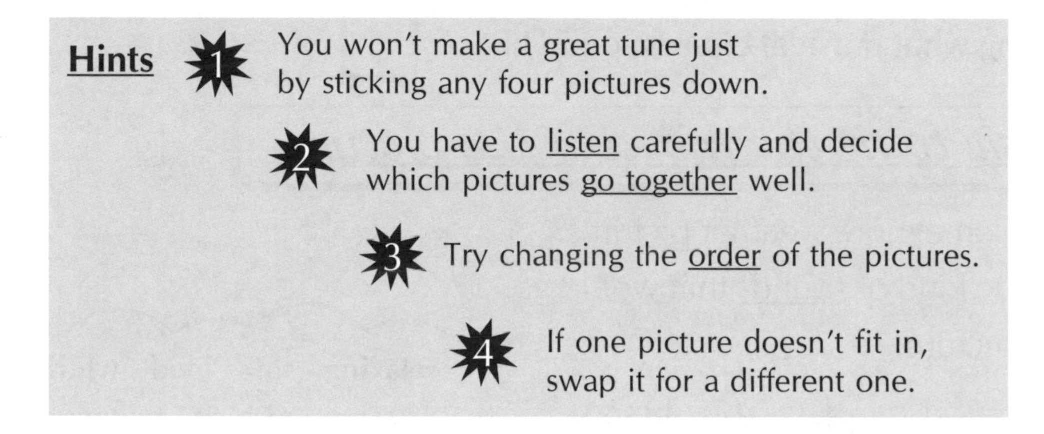

Remember — it's going to be a song with **words**.
That means it has to be something you could sing along to.

When you've got a tune that you're happy with, **draw** the pictures in the boxes below:

Write Your Own Song

Putting words to the tune

Now you need to put **words** to your tune to make it into a **song**.

Hint: Your words have to fit the tune, so practise singing them over the tune. You could try to make your words funny or use them to tell a short story.

Don't rush this bit. Get them just right before you write them down.

Write your words here:

Picture 1 ....

Picture 2 ....

Picture 3 ....

Picture 4 ....

Extra Bits to Try:

1. Make your tune **repeat** itself. (This is called **looping**.)
   What button or command did you use?

   ....

2. Change the **instruments** used to play your song.
   Write down how you did this. (Which menus or commands did you use?)

   ....

   ....

   Which is your favourite instrument? ....

Save your song

Write the name of the file here:

Organising Information

Information means things like phone numbers, dates and times.
Organising information means putting it in a sensible order.

It's Hard to Find Things in a Messy Pile

I've got all my friends' phone numbers on different bits of paper.

I've got all these bits of paper in a messy pile.

It takes ages to find Bob's number.
That's because my information is not organised.

Organised Information is Easier to Use

I've had an idea. I've put the bits of paper in alphabetical order.

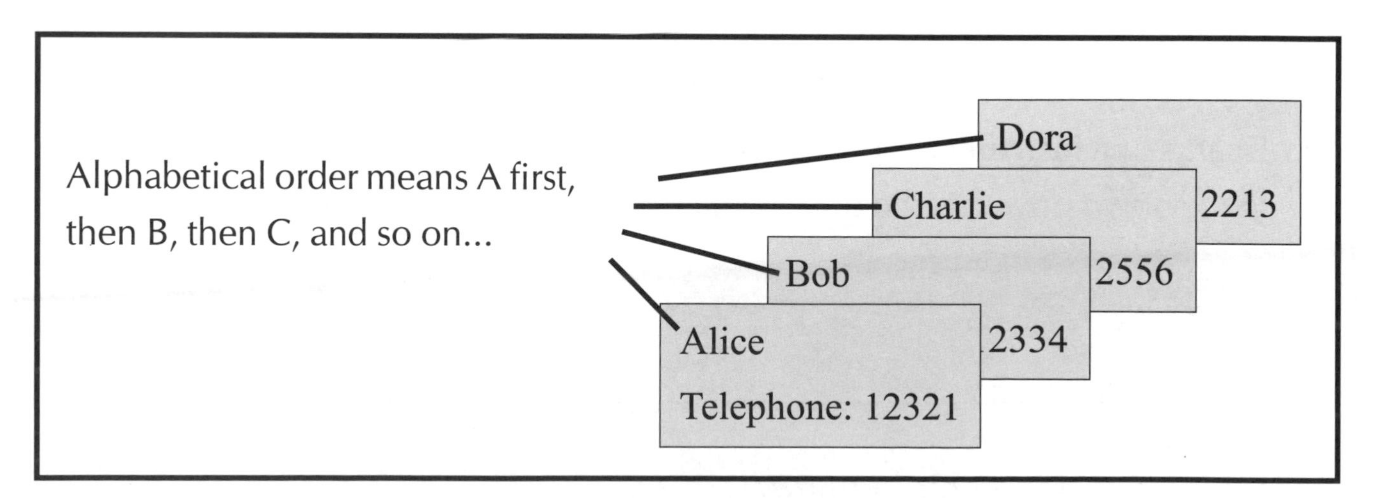

It's much easier to find Bob's number — I just look under "B".
That's because the information is now organised.

Organising Information

① Name three types of information.

1 ....

2 ....

3 ....

② Why is it bad to keep information in messy piles?

....

....

③ Why is it better to have organised information?

....

....

④ Here's one way you can organise information.

Put in the missing letters to finish the words.

A ☐ P H ☐ B ☐ T I ☐ ☐ L

O R D ☐ ☐

E C L A E R A

Record Cards

You can use record cards to organise information.

A record card is just a piece of card with information on it.

Record Cards are a Way to Organise Facts

These record cards are about different monsters.

Each record card has information about one monster.

Name:	Kar Dillak
Lives in:	Swamps
Number of Heads:	3
Can fly:	No

To keep information about ten monsters, you need ten record cards.

Name:	Kar Dillak
Lives in:	Swamps
Number of Heads:	3
Can fly:	No

You can use record cards to answer questions

EXAMPLE: *How many heads does the monster Peekoop have?*
Just find Peekoop's record card and read the answer.

This is Peekoop's card.

Name:	Peekoop
Lives in:	Trees and bushes
Number of Heads:	10
Can fly:	Yes

Peekoop has ten heads.

The information is easy to find if the cards are kept in alphabetical order.

Record Cards

① What can you use record cards for?

....

② How many monsters are on each record card?

....

③ How many record cards do you need for 50 monsters?

....

④ What can you use record cards for?

....

....

⑤ Where does the monster Peekoop live?

....

Records and Fields

Instead of saying 'record card', you can just say 'record' if you want.

Records are Split into Bits called Fields

Records have different fields.

A field contains **one** piece of information.

This record card has four fields.

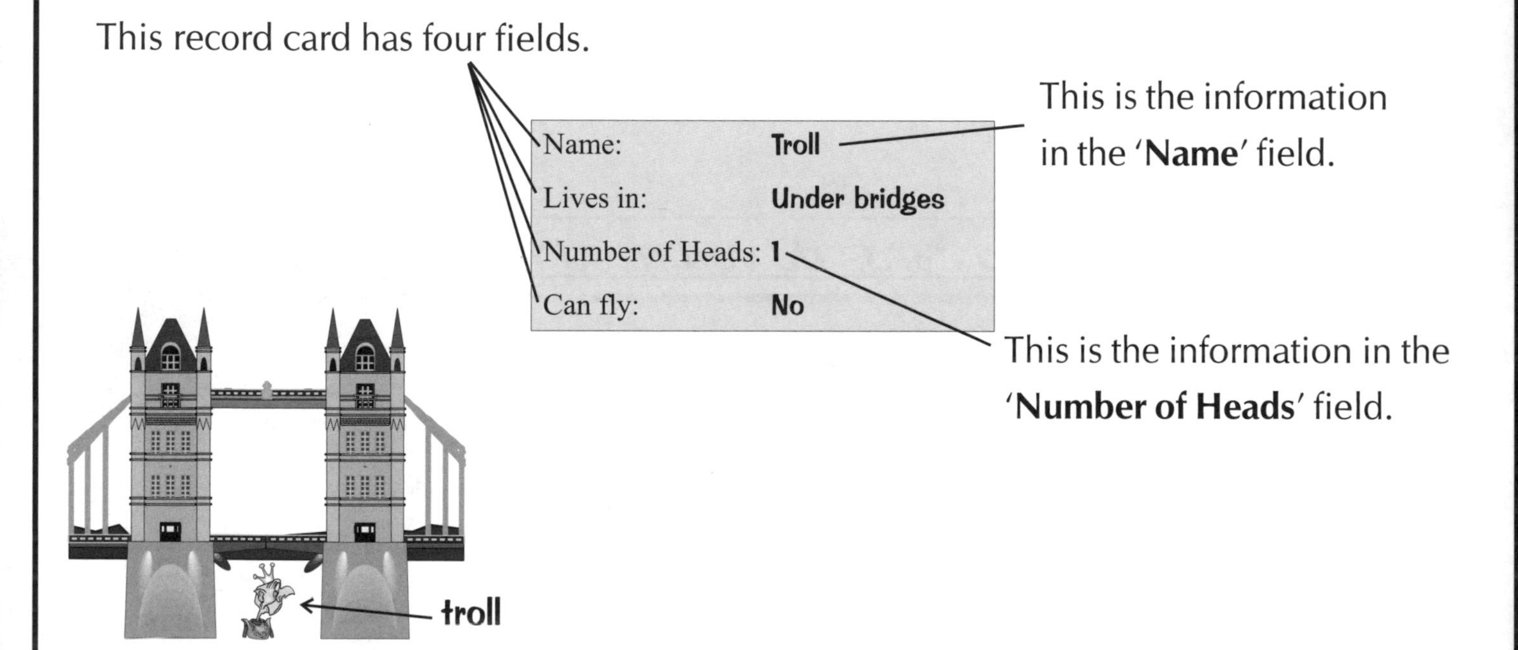

There are Three Different Kinds of Field

Each field can have...

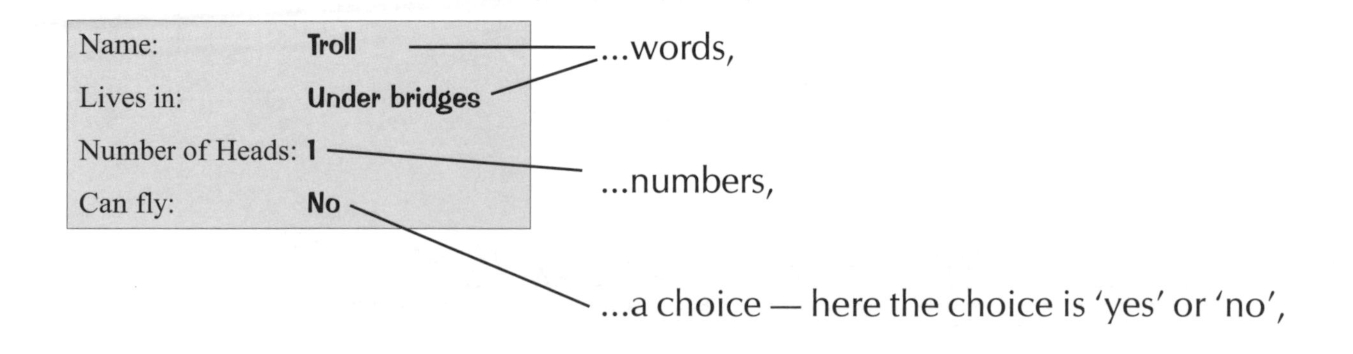

Records and Fields

① *What do records split into?*

....

② *How many pieces of information are in each field?*

....

③ *What three types of information can be in a field?*

1. ....

2. ....

3. ....

④ *Complete this record card for this monster.*

Name:	Urg
Lives in:	....
Number of Heads:	....
Can fly:	No

Databases

Databases are like record cards on the computer. They can be **really** useful.

Databases organise information for you

Databases make it easy to organise information.
This database program is called Junior Viewpoint.

It even looks just like a record card.

Use these buttons to see the records of different monsters.

Use these buttons to go to the first or last record.

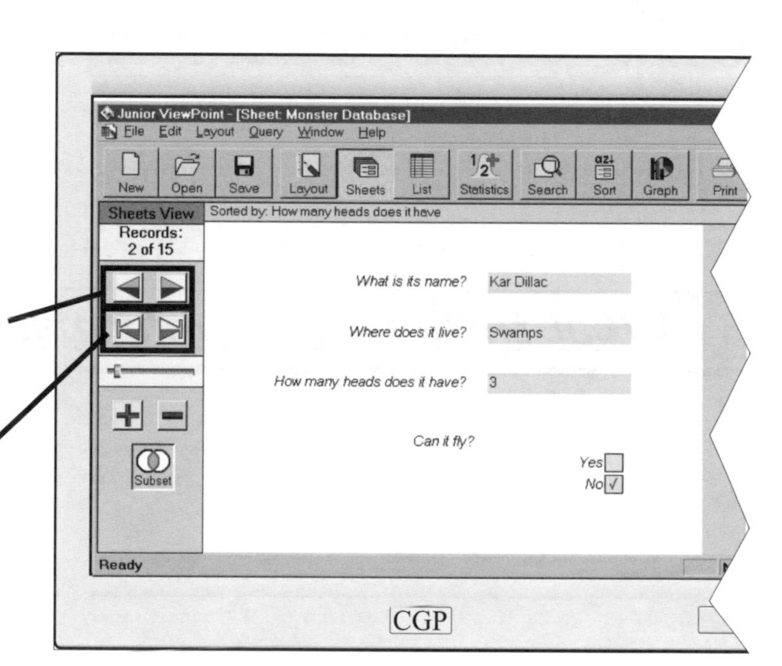

Databases are great because...

1. You can find information quickly.

2. You can arrange records in any order you like.

3. You can draw graphs using your information.

Databases

① What programs help you organise information?

....

② What do these buttons do?

Draw a line from each button to the right description.

Look at the record after this one.

Look at the record before this one.

Look at the last record.

Look at the first record.

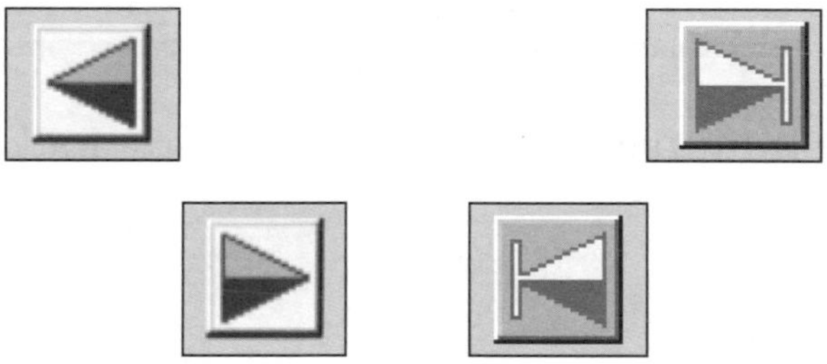

③ Why are databases great?

1. ....

2. ....

3. ....

Adding Records

You sometimes need to add new information.

It's easy to add information to a database

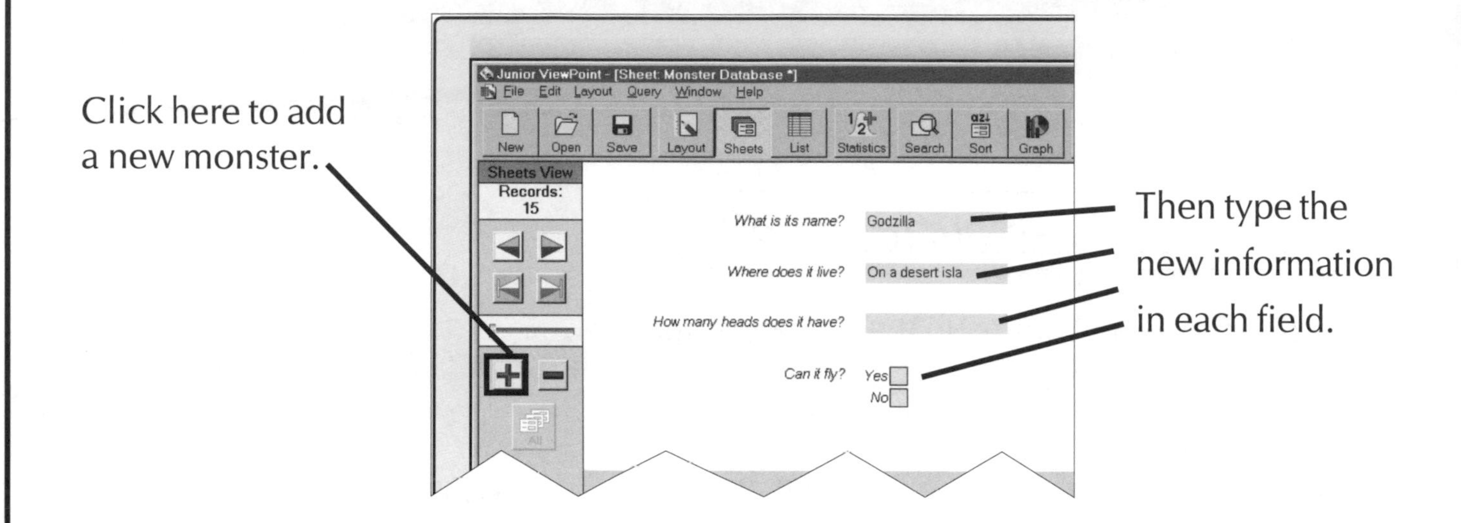

Databases aren't all the same

Sometimes the button to add new information looks a bit different.
It could look like this.

Sometimes there isn't a button at all. So you have to use a menu.

Go to the **Insert Menu**,
and choose **New Record**.

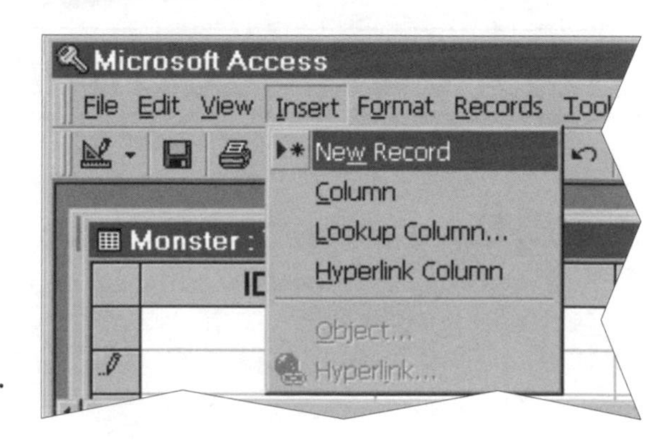

This is a different database program.

Adding Records

① What is the name of your database program?

....

② What could you use a database program for?

Tick the things you could use a database for.

- [ ] Organising information about your record collection.
- [ ] Tidying your bedroom.
- [ ] Organising your friends' telephone numbers.
- [ ] Doing the washing up.
- [ ] Organising information about lots of dinosaurs.

③ How do you add a record if you can't find the button?

Draw a pair of horns on the best answer, like this.

Panic.

Use a menu.

Close the program.

Make a Database

You will need to set up a database program, using fields chosen during this exercise.
Note: The field **Birthday Month** should be a **number** field.

In this project you will:

You will put information about everyone in your class into a database.

Make a question sheet

Follow these points to make a great question sheet.

1. Start with these three questions:

   What is your first name?
   In which month is your birthday?
   Which day of the month is your birthday?

2. Add four more questions.
   Your questions should have different kinds of answers.

   Examples:

   1. Some questions should ask for a **word** — like *"What is your dad's name?"*
   2. Some should ask for **numbers** — like *"How many pets do you have?"*
   3. Some questions should give a **choice** of two things — like *"Are you are boy or a girl?"*

3. Write the questions on a piece of card.

   1 What is your first name?
   2. In which month is your birthday?
   3. Which day of the month is your birthday?
   4. Are you a boy or a girl?
   5. What is your favourite food?
   6. How tall are you (in cm)?
   7. Do you have any pets (yes or no)?

   This is my question sheet.

Make a Database

Computer Activity

Ask your questions

Ask everyone in your class the questions on your sheet.

Write down the answers on a separate sheet of paper.

1 Andy	1 Caroline	1 Simon
2. July	2. August	2. February
3. 3	3. 20	3. 4
4. boy	4. girl	4. boy
5. curry	5. chips	5. bacon
6. 130 cm	6. 114 cm	6. 125 cm
7. no	7. yes	7. no

Add all the information to your database

This is the fun bit.

You have to add all the information you collected to the database.

Look at page 42 if you can't remember how to do it.

When you type in the **Birthday Month**, use these codes.

January = 1	April = 4	July = 7	October = 10
February = 2	May = 5	August = 8	November = 11
March = 3	June = 6	September = 9	December = 12

Now use the ▶ and ◀ buttons to look at all the different records in your database.

Don't forget to save your database

Write the filename of your database here.

Putting Things in Order

It's easy to put things in alphabetical order.

Or put numbers in order — smallest first, biggest last.

Sorting is Cool

Putting records in order is called **sorting**.

Sorting a database is easy.

1. **Press the sort button.**
   It'll look like one of these.

   az↓ Sort

   A Z ↓

2. **Choose a field** to sort.

   You could sort the **height** field — to put people in order of height.

   You could sort the **name** field — to put people in alphabetical order.

Sort Your Database to Answer Questions

You can answer questions like these by sorting your database.

Who is the **tallest** person in the class?

Who is the **shortest** person in the class?

Who has the **most** pets?

Whose name comes **first** alphabetically?

Putting Things in Order

① *Sort these lists.*

Put these numbers **in order**. Start with the **smallest** number.

127 2 28 99 67 33

....

Put these names in **alphabetical order**.

Claire Andy Bill Joanne

....

② *How would you do this?*

You have a database about animals. It has these fields:

Name **Height** **Number of legs** **Favourite food** **Maximum speed**

Which field would you **sort** to answer these questions?
Write the name of the field here.

Question	***Field to Sort***
Which animal has the most legs?	....
Which is the fastest animal?	....
Which animal's name comes first alphabetically?	....
Which animal is the tallest?	....
Which animal is the shortest?	....

Looking for Things

You can find things in a database by doing a search.

You could search for all the people with blue eyes. It's easy.

Searching a database is Easy

This is how you find all the people with **blue eyes**:

1. Press the **Search** button.

   It'll look something like this. — Search

2. Choose the **field**. Here it'll be **Eye colour**.

   You may have to click on the field or choose from a list of fields.

   In Junior Viewpoint you click on the field.

   List | Statistics | Search | Sort | Gra

   Name · Age · Sex · Eye colour · Hair colour · Height

3. Type in the eye colour you want to search for. Here it's "**blue**".

You can Search for Answers to Questions

Searching a database makes it easy to answer questions too.

You can answer questions like these:

Whose favourite food is curry?
Who doesn't have any pets?
Who is exactly 130 cm tall?

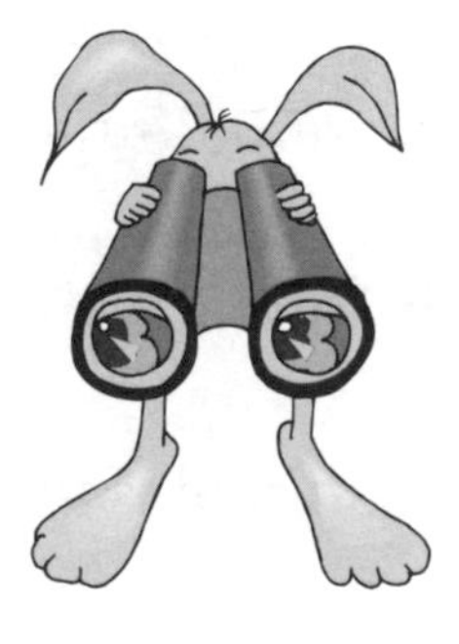

Looking for Things

① Which is the Search Button?

Draw an eggshell around the right one.

② How would you find this?

I have a database about pop stars. It has these fields.

Name **Year they were born** **Town where they live**
Colour of Hair **Biggest hit** **Favourite colour**

I want to answer some questions. For each question:

work out **which field I should search**,

then work out **what words** I should **look for.**

1. Which pop stars have black hair?

   Field: Colour of Hair .... **Look for:** black ....

2. Whose favourite colour is yellow?

   Field: .... **Look for:** ....

3. Whose biggest hit was "Bubblegum"?

   Field: .... **Look for:** ....

4. Which pop stars live in Manchester?

   Field: .... **Look for:** ....

Drawing Graphs

Drawing bar charts with a database is brilliant.
And it's quicker than drawing them yourself.

Bar Charts Use One Field

This is a bar chart. It was drawn on a computer.

It uses the field **Eye Colour**.

It shows how many people have which colour eyes.

Twenty people have brown eyes.

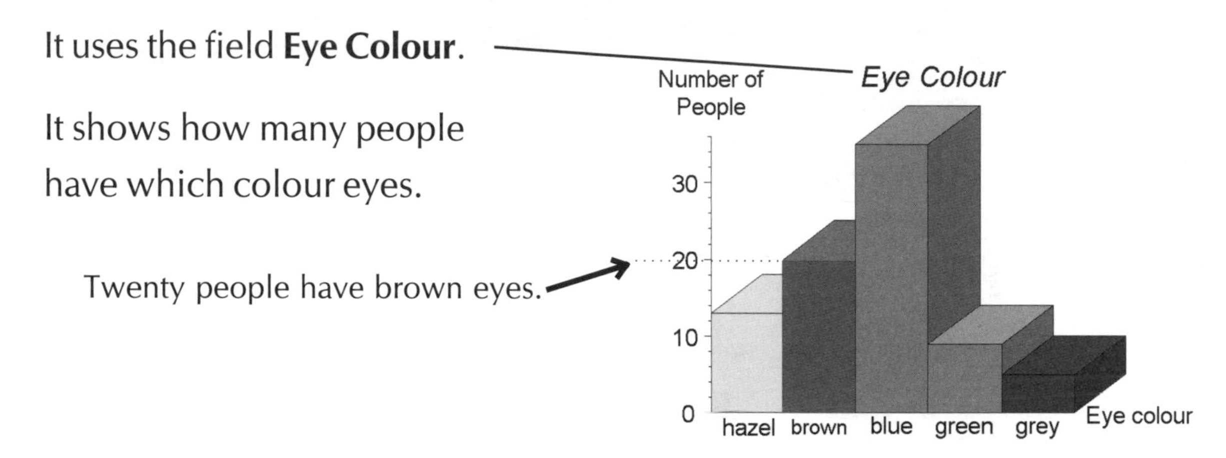

Make a Bar Chart — It's Easy

1. Press the **Graphs** button.

2. Choose **Bar Chart**.

3. Choose which **field** you want to use.

Choose this from a drop-down list.

Drawing Graphs

① Read these Bar Charts.

Answer the questions using these bar charts.

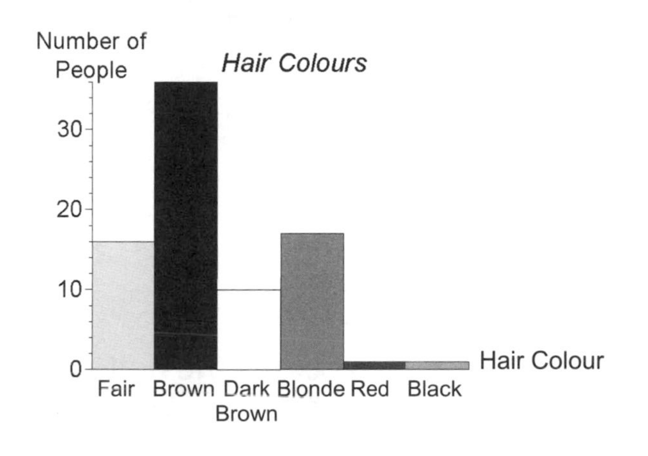

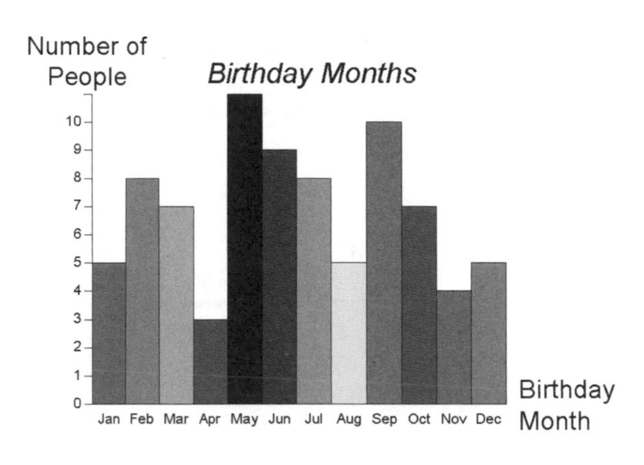

1. How many people have blonde hair? ....

2. How many people have their birthday in April? ....

② Draw a Bar Chart.

Draw a bar chart to show what pets people own. Use the information in this table.

Type of pet	Number of people
dog	10
cat	8
budgie	7
hamster	9
goat	3

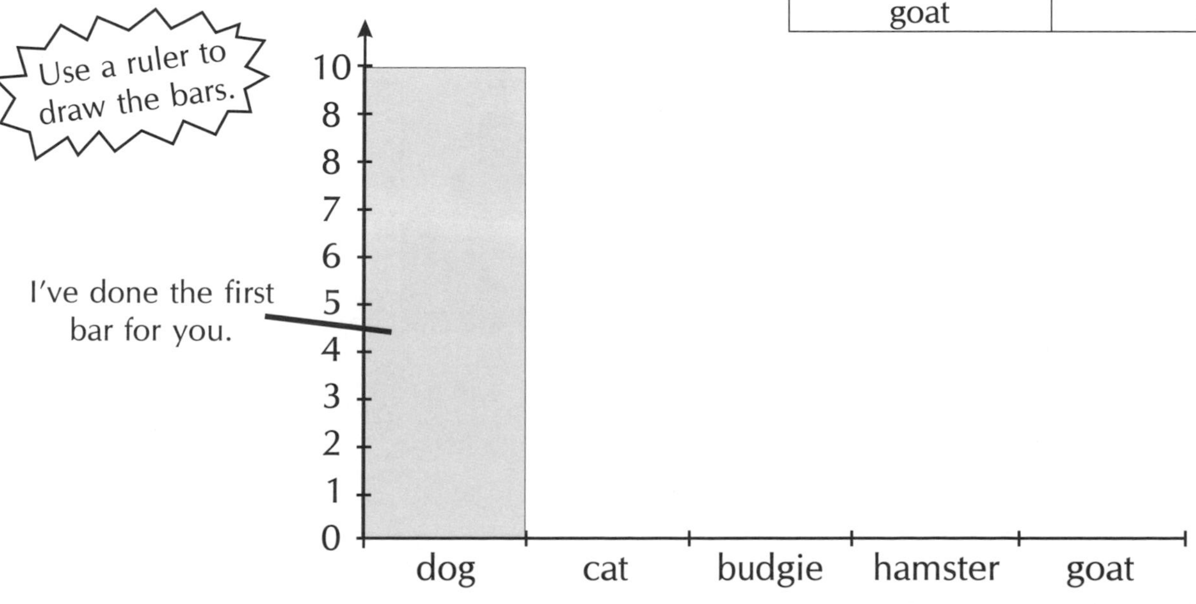

Computer Activity

Use Your Database

You will need the class database you made on pages 44-45.

In this project you will:

Make a birthday chart for your class.

First draw a bar chart

You're going to make a 'Birthday Chart' for some of your class.

This shows the number of people with their birthday in each month.

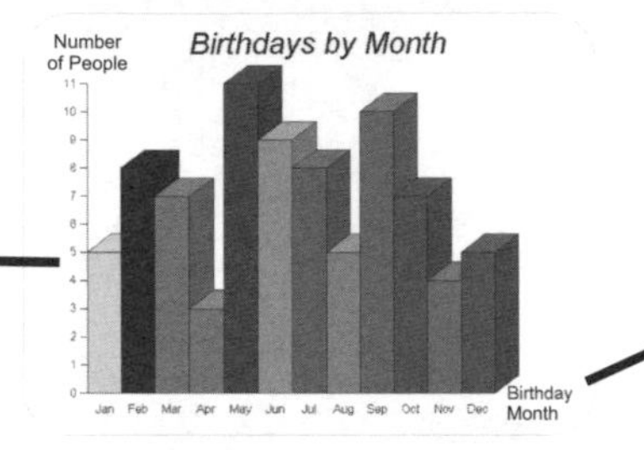

The months go along the bottom.

How to do it

1. **Open** the database about your class you made earlier.
2. **Sort** your database using the **Birthday Month** field.
   (This is so that January comes first, then February, then March,...)
3. **Draw a bar chart** using the **Birthday Month** field.

Make it look nice

You can **change** parts of the graph to make it look good.
To change what's written, double-click on the word.

① Change the title. "**Birthdays by Month**" is better than this.

② Change the labels.
"**Number of People**" is better.

③ Change these numbers to months.
Use: Jan for January,
Feb for February,
Mar for March,...

④ Get rid of things you don't need — like this.

Use Your Database

Now make a list of all the birthdays in each month

Pick **one** month. You're going to make a list of all the birthdays in that month.

Search your database

1. You need to find all the people with a birthday in the month you've picked.
2. **Search** your database. Use the **Birthday Month** field.

Sort the birthdays into the right order

1. Now you need to put all the birthdays in the right order.
2. **Sort** the records. Use the **Birthday Day** field.

Look at all the records in List View

Look at all the records at the same time by pressing the **List View** button.

You can use a menu to do this if you like.

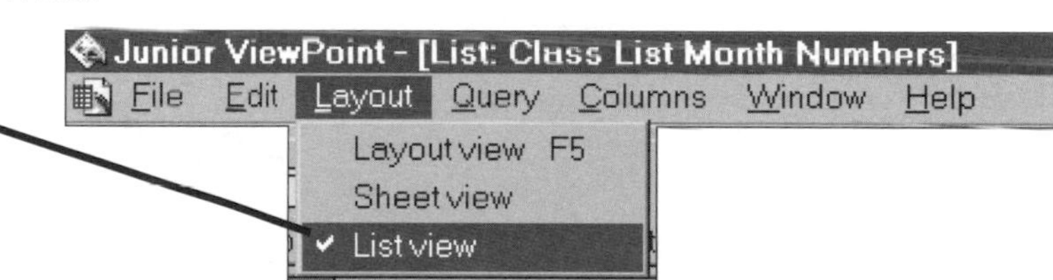

You'll see something like this.

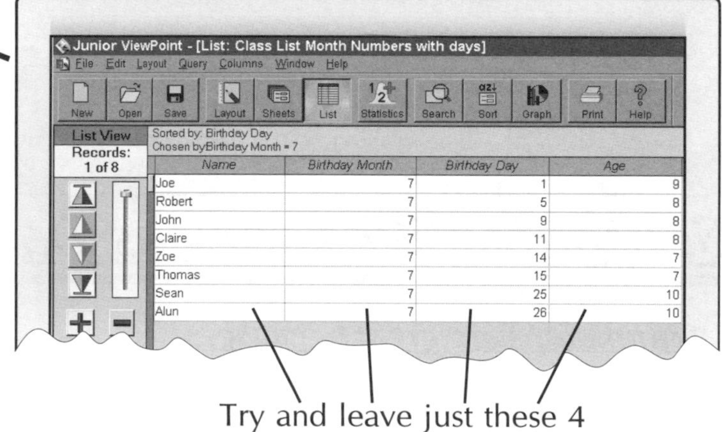

Try and leave just these 4 columns on your birthday list.

Print out your birthday list

Put it on your classroom wall.

Now you can remember everyone's birthday.

What are Simulations?

1) Simulation is a big word. It means "pretend".
2) With simulations you can pretend to fly a plane or ride a motorbike — on the computer.

There are Different Kinds of Simulation

Here are some examples:

1) A flight game where you fly an aeroplane.

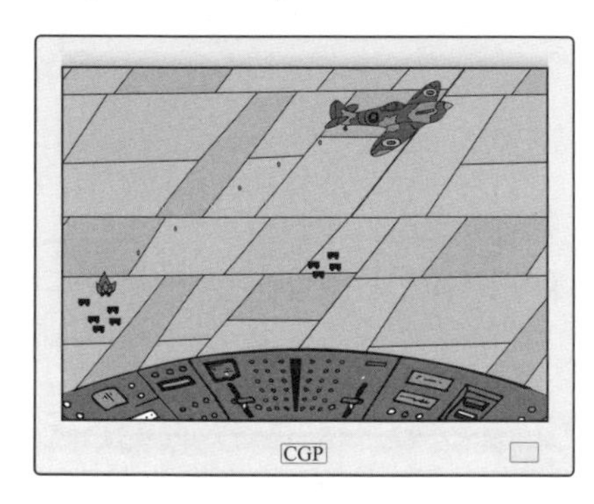

2) A virtual pet (like a *Tamagotchi*).

3) A program to design a new car.

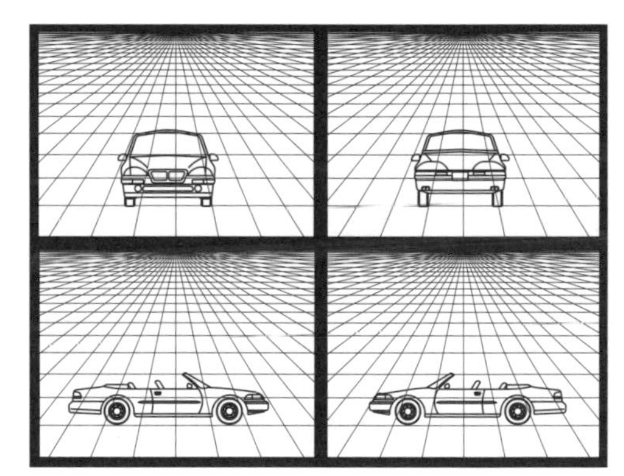

Computer Simulations have Loads of Uses

Simulations are great because:

1) You can try impossible things.
2) You can train pilots.
3) You can test new inventions.

But there are problems:

1) Simulations are often too simple.
2) They can be very expensive.

What are Simulations?

① What does "Simulation" mean?

....

② Give three examples of simulations.

1. ....

2. ....

3. ....

③ Why are Simulations Great?

1. ....

2. ....

3. ....

④ What are the Problems?

1. ....

2. ....

Simulation — that's a big fancy word...

This is how you say it: *SIM-YOO-LAY-SHUN*. Say it out loud now.

Making Choices

In most simulations, you have to make choices.
The choices you make can change what happens.

Examples of the Choices You can Make

With virtual pets you can choose:

- what to feed them (and how much)
- how often to play with them
- how often to clean the cage out

These things change how well your pet grows, and how happy it is.

In flight simulations you can choose:

- how fast to fly
- how much to turn
- how high to fly

These things change how well you fly.

In adventure games you can choose:

- which way to go
- which sword to use in a fight
- who to speak to

These things change how quickly you solve the puzzle, or how long you survive.

Making Choices

1a What choices can you make in a virtual pet program?

1. ....

2. ....

3. ....

1b What can you change by making different choices?

☐ Whether the animal is a dog or a cat.

☐ How happy the animal is.

☐ How well the animal grows.

2 What affects how well you fly in a flight game?

1. ....

2. ....

3. ....

3 These are some choices from an adventure game.

The things on the left change the things on the right.

For each choice, draw a line to one of the results. I've done one for you.

Choice	Result
How much money you pick up	What you can find out
Which sword you use in a fight	Whether you win the fight
Who you speak to	What you can buy

Finding Patterns

This page is about working out what difference each choice makes.

I kept four virtual plants for a month.
I gave each plant different amounts of water.

Plant	How often I watered it	How tall it grew
A	not at all	10 cm
B	once a week	15 cm
C	once a day	25 cm
D	twice a day	30 cm

The Pattern: The more often I watered a plant, the taller it grew.

Write down each Choice you make

When you make a choice, always:

1) Write down clearly what *you did*.
2) Write down what *happened*.

This makes it easy to see *patterns*.

It's good to write clearly because:

1) It's easier for you to read it.
2) It's easier for your teacher to read it.

How to get the Best Results:

1) Do a fair test — only change one thing at a time.
2) Repeat everything — to see if you get the same results.

Finding Patterns

① How should you keep track of each choice you make?

1. ....

2. ....

② How does this help?

....

③ Look at these results and complete the pattern.

I am playing an adventure game, and I'm in a difficult fight.
I try using different-length swords — these are the results:

Sword	Result of fight
 (shortest sword)	I lose.
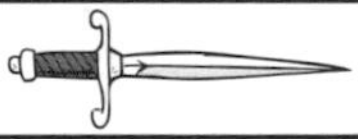 (short sword)	Draw.
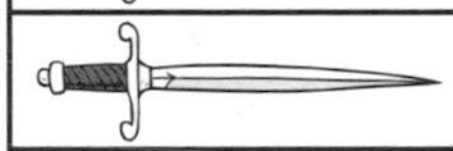 (longer sword)	I win but I'm hurt badly.
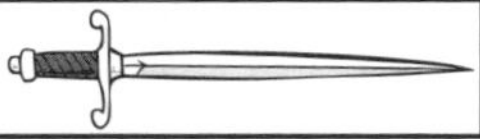 (longest sword)	I win easily.

Ring the right word below.

The Pattern: I am more likely to win if I use a LONGER / SHORTER sword.

④ How do you get the best results?

1. ....

2. ....

Guessing What Will Happen

Look at What's Happened Before

VIRTUAL PET EXAMPLE:

Question: My virtual dog usually wags his tail when I play with him. What do you think will happen next time I play with him?

Look at what happened last time. It'll probably happen next time.

Answer: *I think he will wag his tail*.

Test it Out

Looks like I guessed right...

Follow the Pattern (if there is one)

1) Look at the pattern.
2) Follow it a bit further and say what you think will happen.
3) Test it out.

FLIGHT GAME EXAMPLE:

Question: The faster you fly the plane, the quicker you run out of fuel. How long will the fuel last if the plane flies *really fast*?

Answer:

1) The pattern is: "*The faster you fly the plane, the quicker you run out of fuel*."
2) Follow the pattern — if the plane goes really fast, the fuel will run out quickly.
3) Fly the plane really fast. See if you were right.

Guessing What Will Happen

① What should you do to work out what'll happen?

....

② Look at these results and say what will happen next.

I've designed a car. I have tested it using a computer simulation.
Each time the car goes round a corner, a wheel falls off.

What do you think will happen next time it goes round a corner?

....

③ How can you test out your idea?

....

④ Have a go at this one if you've got time...

The quicker the car goes round a corner, the more wheels fall off.

What do you think will happen if it goes round a corner really quickly?

☐ A: one wheel will fall off

☐ B: all four wheels will fall off

☐ C: all the wheels will stay on

What is E-mail?

E-mail lets you send messages to people with a computer.
Everyone uses it now — it's much quicker than posting a letter.

What's so good about E-mail?

E-mail's great because:

1. It's really quick.
2. It's cheap.
3. You can use it in different places.

But E-mail's a pain because:

1. It's not secret — other people might read it.
2. It's not permanent (doesn't last for ever).
3. You have to type.

E-mail Addresses Look Like This:

name@blah.blah.uk

Write the e-mail address here.

Send other people copies of the e-mail by putting their addresses here.

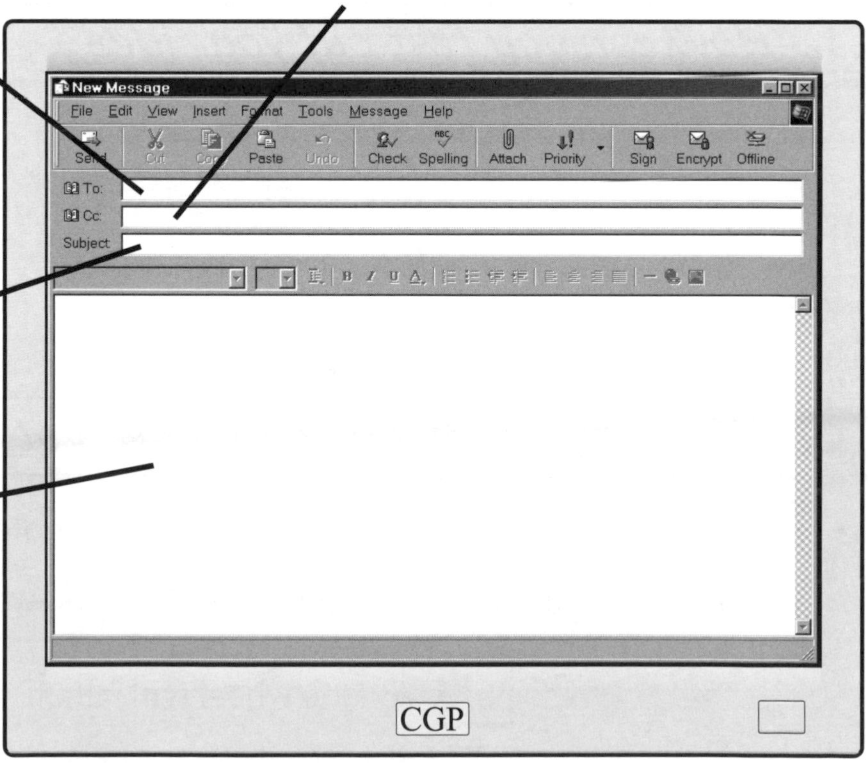

The "subject" means "what it's about". Write it here.

Write your message in this big white space.

Once you've finished your message, you just need to send it.
All you do is press the send button and the message will go on its way.

First Bits of E-mail

① Why is E-mail great?

1 ....

2 ....

3 ....

② Why can E-mail be a pain?

1 ....

2 ....

3 ....

③ What does "Subject" mean?

....

....

④ What is the box next to Cc: for?

....

....

Reading E-mail

Getting new e-mails is really exciting.

New E-mails go in the Inbox

The Inbox is where to look for new messages.

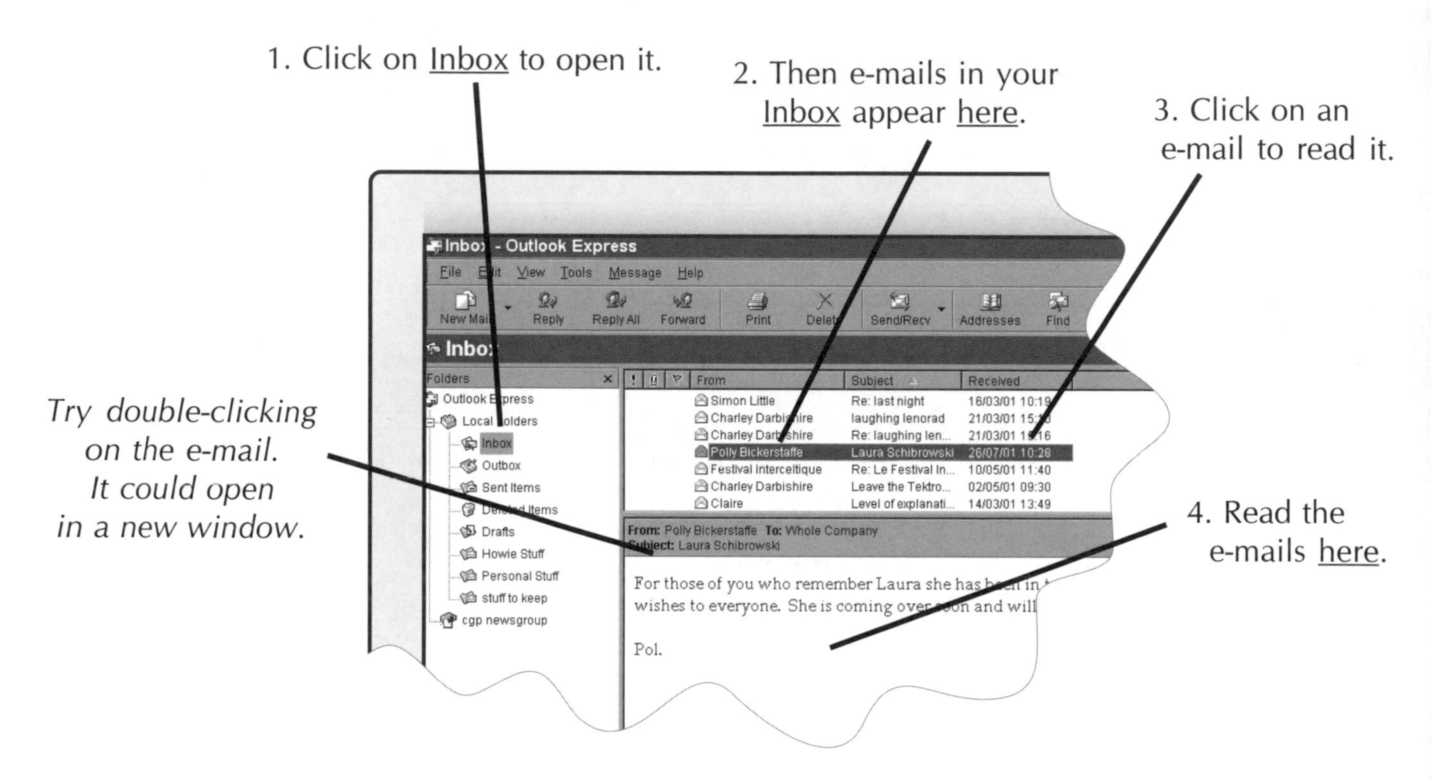

This e-mail program is Outlook Express.
(All e-mail programs do the same jobs, even if they look different.)

You can print E-mails you want to keep

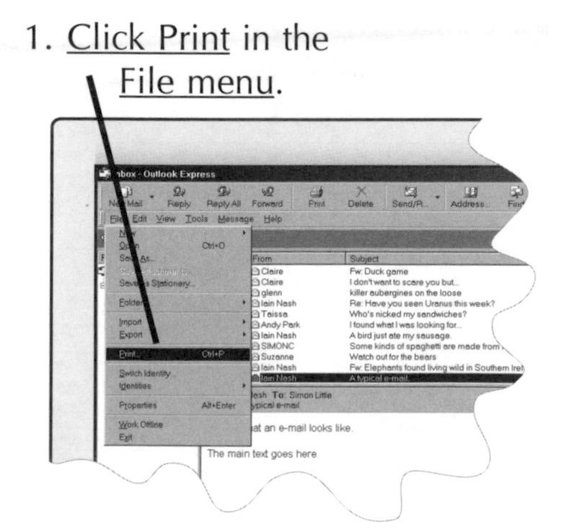

REMEMBER — click on Cancel to go Back.

2. A new box will appear. It will look a bit like this. Click on OK.

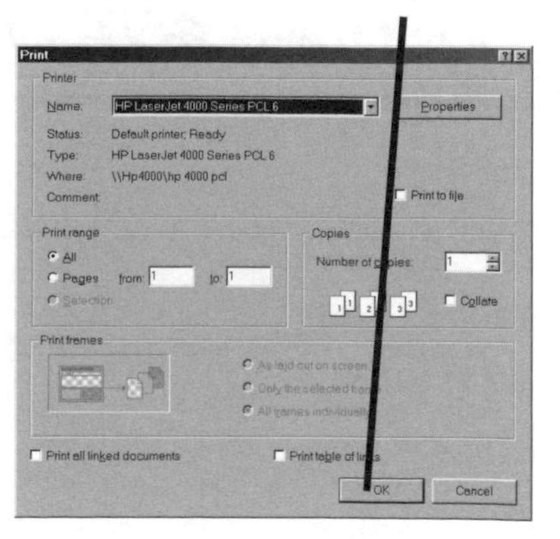

Reading E-mail

① Where do new e-mails go?

....

....

② How do you open the inbox?

....

....

③ How do you print an e-mail?

1 ....

....

....

....

2 ....

....

Replying to E-mail

When someone sends you a message, you'll want to reply.
Reply means "write back".

Sending a Reply is Dead Easy

Replying is easy. You don't have to type the person's address in.
The computer does it all for you.

1. Click on reply.

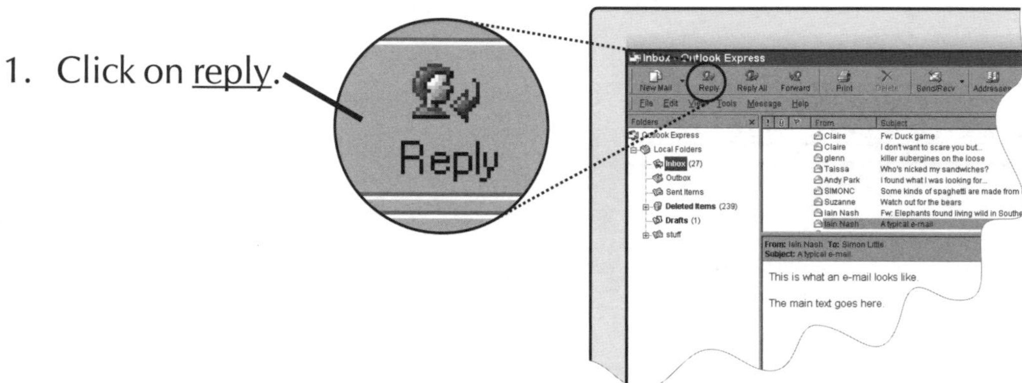

2. And then you get a window a bit like this.

Re: This is what the email is about
File Edit View Insert Format Tools Message Help
Send Cut Copy Paste Undo Check Spelling Attach Priority Sign Encrypt Offline
To: Georgina Western
Cc:
Subject: Re: This is what the email is about
Book Antiqua 10

Hi Georgie,

This is my reply.

Claire

----- Original Message -----
From: Georgina Western
To: Claire@emailaddress.co.uk
Sent: 04 April 2001 09:00
Subject: Re: This is what the email is about

This is the original message from me.

Georgie

CGP

3. Write your message here.

4. This is the old message. It's the one you're replying to.

   (Not all e-mail programs put the old message in like this.)

5. Click on send to send the e-mail.

Replying to E-mail

① What does "reply" mean?

....

② Match the words to the pictures.

Draw a line from each label to the right bit of the picture.

1. Click this button to reply to Georgina's message.
2. This is the message from Georgina.

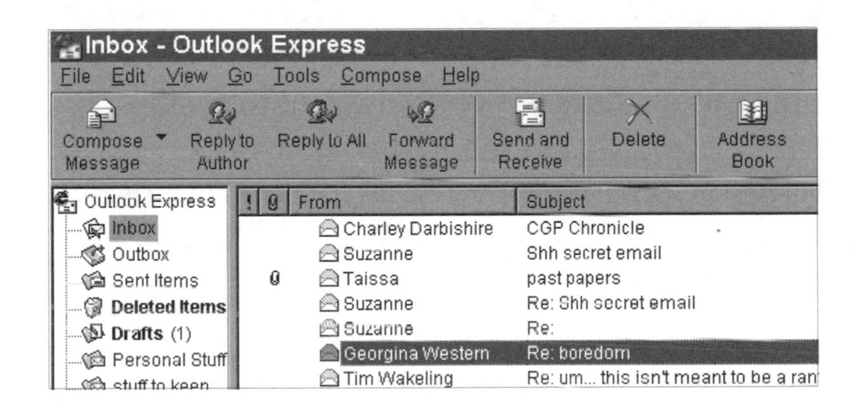

③ What happens when you click on reply?

Tick the right answer.

☐ A window appears for you to type a message.

☐ The program closes.

④ When you've written your reply, how do you send it?

....

⑤ Do you always get the old message in your reply?

....

Sending an E-mail

It's easy to send an e-mail. Just type in the address.

There are Four Stages to Sending an E-mail

1. Write the address.
2. Write the subject.
3. Write your message.
4. Press the send button.

This is the trickiest bit.
You have to get the address exactly right.

Remember — subject is what it's about.

Don't Worry about Getting Things Wrong

If you do use the wrong e-mail address, two things can happen:

1. It goes to the wrong person.
   Never mind, they'll probably ignore it.

2. You get a message saying there's no such address.
   Don't worry — these messages are from computers, not people.

Keep E-mail Addresses in the Address Book

Using an address book is really helpful:

1. You can keep all your e-mail addresses in one place.
2. You can send messages without typing the e-mail addresses. Hurray!

To send a message:

1. Click on the person you want to send it to.
2. Click on "Send Mail".
3. A window will appear.
4. Type your message as normal.

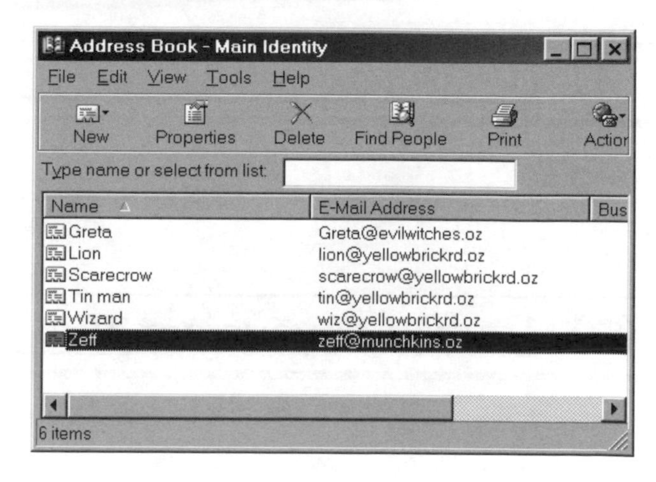

Sending an E-mail

① What are the four steps to sending an e-mail?

1. ....

2. ....

3. ....

4. ....

② Will the world end if you type the wrong address?

....

③ Which of these is the Address Book?

Circle the correct window.

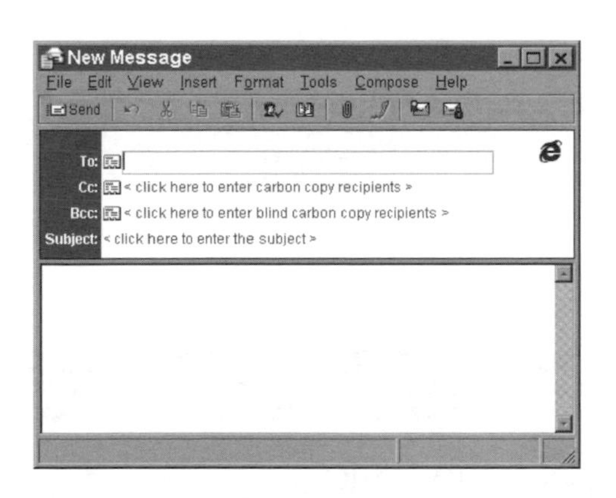

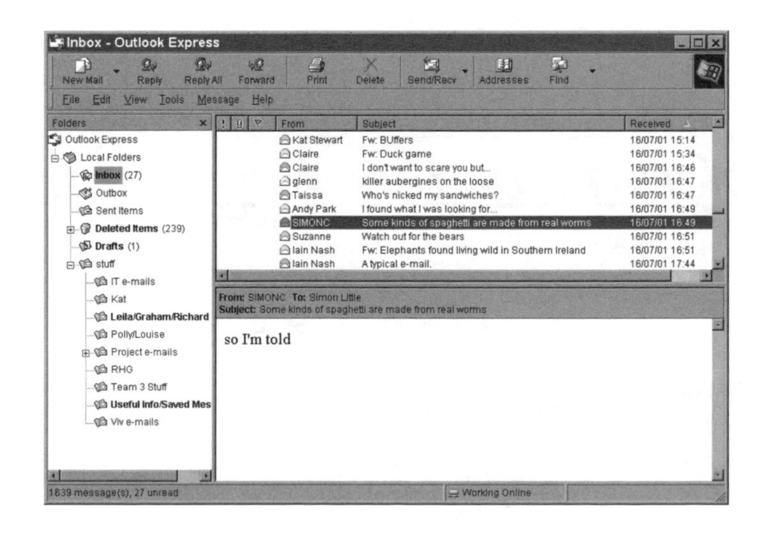

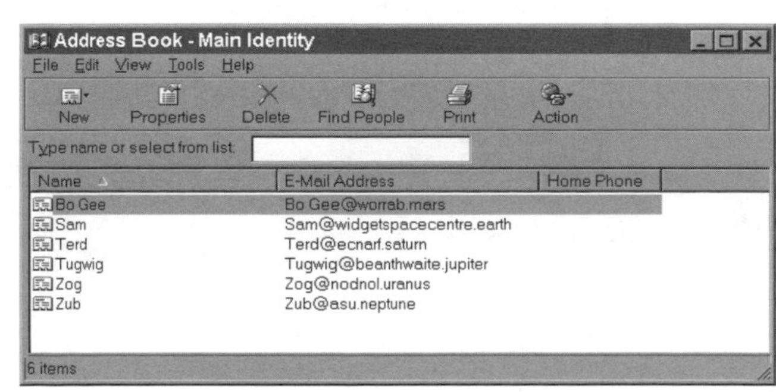

Attachments

You can attach stuff to e-mails

It's great. You can send a picture to your friends or send a song to your Gran. It's just ACE.

Here's what you do:

1) Write a message.

2) Click on the paperclip.

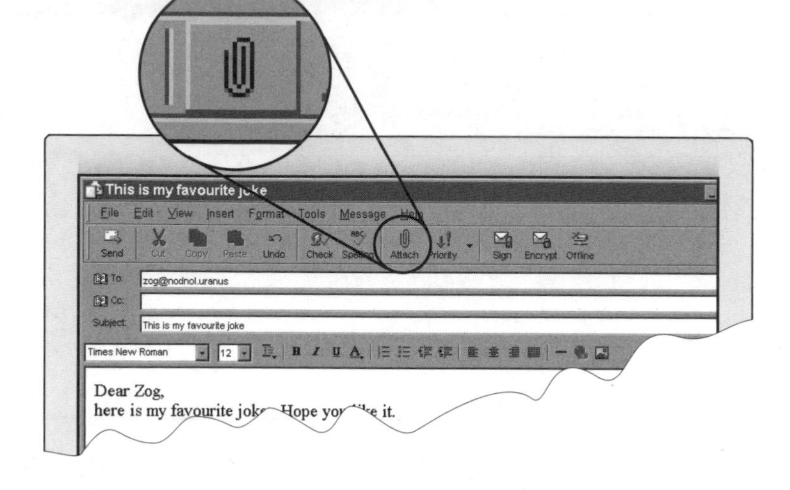

3) A window will appear...

4) Click on the file you want to attach.

You need to find the right folder first.

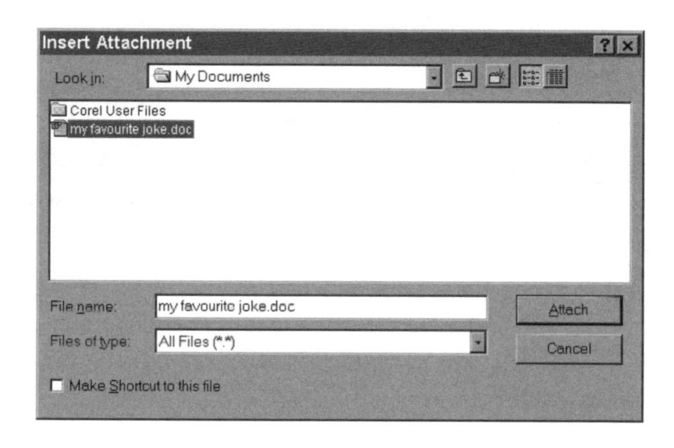

5) Click "Attach". Easy.

You can attach sounds, pictures or text files

This is what it looks like...